The Complete Soaring Guide

Ann Welch

The Complete **SOARING** Guide

Ann Welch

A & C Black · London

First published 1986
by A & C Black (Publishers) Ltd
35 Bedford Row, London, WC1R 4JH

Welch, Ann
   The complete soaring guide.
   1. Gliding and soaring
   I. Title
   797.5'5   GV764

   ISBN 0–7136–5540–2

Design: Janet Simmonett

Typeset in 10pt Helvetica Light by August
Filmsetting, St. Helens
Printed and bound in England by Hazell,
Watson & Viney Ltd, Aylesbury

Acknowledgements
The author wishes gratefully to acknowledge
permission to reproduce the following
photographs:
British Gliding Association: p.41
Cambridge Instruments: p.36
Glasflugel: pp. 17, 29, 113
Field Tech Ltd: p.23 (bottom)
Flight: p.101
Paul Schweizer: pp. 51, 95 (left), 115 (top left),
   139, 142
Peter Selinger: p.44
Colin Street: p.138
Frank Irving: pp. 3, 79, 82, 83 (bottom)
All other photographs (except those on pp.
50, 65 and 93 which carry no identification)
and illustrations are by the author.

Contents

The three white birds, by which sailplane pilots
recognise each other all over the world.

Introduction

What are the attractions of gliding, or flying without an engine? Of risking ending up in a muddy field while, with power, you can fly where you want and arrive on schedule—at least most of the time. All over the world there are pilots who want to fly sailplanes and nothing else; and many have continued to do so for forty years or more—why?

There are many reasons. For some pilots it is the challenge of taking on the elemental forces that make the weather, of searching out the air that is rising and escaping from air that tries to force them back to earth. It is a form of combat that brings great satisfaction when you win, and does no harm—except perhaps to your pride—when you lose. For others, the pleasure of soaring is simply its beauty: to fly quietly over an ever-changing sunlit land, dotted with the deep shadows of bright clouds above, is a magnificent experience. There are also pilots who, all their lives, have been fascinated by the mastery of the birds, and now delight in soaring with them—though on one occasion an eagle did attack a sailplane intruding into its mountain territory!

Maybe it is for none of these reasons that you will, or already have, become a soaring fanatic; maybe you just want a refreshing change at weekends from a stuffy weekday office, or perhaps a friend just takes you along to help him put his sailplane together. But even if you start gliding, and for any reason do not continue, you will have had a glimpse of a new and different world.

Soaring began as a sport some sixty years ago, with crude home-made gliders which hardly soared at all. So the challenge then was simply to stay airborne, to defeat gravity for just one more minute between the hill top from which the glider took off, down into the valley. But even an extra minute was little compensation for the hour or more needed to carry the glider back up the hill again. Then it was discovered that when there was a good wind blowing up the hill, this would support the glider for longer—provided it flew in the narrow band of lift above the edge of the hill. Pilots soon became brilliant at using every gust and gully to their advantage, and they built large, light, and very slow sailplanes to help them.

It was nearly another decade before pilots could escape from the hills, however much they loved flying among them. One day a German pilot, Max Kegel, was sucked up by a large cumulus cloud—which was rapidly developing into a cumulo-nimbus (cu-nb). Finally he fell out of the storm, turned his height into distance, and landed 55 km away to make the world's first true cross-country flight.

It still took a few years to learn about thermals, inspite of pilots seeing birds circling up from the warm valleys. But when it was appreciated that it was thermals that created the cumulus, this was the start of cross-country soaring as we know it. For the next few years, until the start of the Second World War, distance flying was all that mattered: to fly further and further, exploring new country, new clouds, and to land in the evenings in new places. This was perfection—except that it took all night to retrieve the glider and drive home.

As sailplane performance continued to improve, a few pilots realised that it was becoming more sensible to fly to a turn point and to try to soar back again. But this required the pilot to fly crosswind or into wind, instead of only downwind. For this the old, slow gliders would not be good enough, and faster ones would need to be built.

In 1948 the first triangular speed record was established at a world championship; now most soaring flights are triangles. For some years the triangles became larger—up to 500 km; then with the advent of glass-fibre sailplanes faster speeds were achieved. Today triangles are both fast and large. The world record for the 100 km triangle is 195 km/h and the biggest triangle flown is 1307 km.

With such progress it might seem that there is no achievement left that is within reach of the ordinary pilot, but the intricate behaviour of the air is still not yet fully understood. Soaring is attractive because every flight is different and is an exploration in its own right. It is something worth going for.

How to get started

In most countries flying is carried out from gliding clubs, which provide the launch equipment, trailer parks, and whatever else is needed. In the United States soaring is more of an individual activity, because of the greater distances, and the availability of towing aeroplanes and of small airfields from which to fly. Each country has a National Gliding or Soaring Association to look after the sport, and these will provide lists of clubs, schools etc. (see page 138).

There are a few people who think that gliding, and soaring, is something magical and not for them. This is not true, since anyone who can drive a car can learn to fly a sailplane; and only normal fitness is needed. If you think you might like soaring but are not sure, go and have a flight at a club or school, or with a friend. Choose a day when the weather is fine, and you will get a good idea of how enjoyable even a simple ten-minute flight can be.

If you are now tempted to do more, it is best to go on a basic course for one or two weeks, and live at a club with other beginners. This would still not commit you to more than the cost of the course, but it would con-centrate your training so that you can progress faster than if you fly only occasionally.

Training flights are made in two-seat sailplanes with dual control so that the instructor can show you what to do— or take over if you get into a muddle. In due course, perhaps after only two weeks of flying regularly, you will be good enough to fly solo—and you will be a pilot. A few people stop flying once they have flown solo, thinking they have achieved all they wanted, but they do not yet know anything about the fun and satisfaction of soaring.

Using this book

This book is divided into three parts which can be read in any order, depending on your interests. The first part is about the sailplane itself, the second concerns learning to fly, and the third part covers the many aspects of soaring. This ranges from making your first cross-country flight, through to competition flying, with a look at the weather and map reading navigation in between. The book is not intended in any way to replace the club or school instructor, but will look at those techniques and concepts which the new pilot may find difficult to remember when he is learning to fly. For many people there seem to be so many new actions competing for concentration at the same time. As well as giving the interested newcomer a broad picture of the whole sport of gliding and soaring, it is hoped that this book will act as a useful reference to the pilot throughout all his early flying career—and even later as a refresher for that infrequently used knowledge.

The Italian Calif high performance two-seater.

Part 1: The sailplane

A sailplane may be called an aeroplane without an engine, but that is where the similarity ends. The pure white slender-winged birds of today are the result of years of refined design work with a single objective: to produce a machine with the flattest possible glide.

If you look at any sailplane its most characteristic features are the long, narrow wings. Most sailplanes have wing spans of 15 metres (49.2 ft), with top competition sailplanes having wing spans of up to 24.5 m (80.4 ft), while the chord of the wing (its width) is often less than 1 m. This relation-ship of span to chord is called *aspect ratio*. Compare the aspect ratios of the three sailplanes (page 12) with that of a typical small aeroplane.

Most single-seater sailplanes are built of glass fibre, but many school two-seaters are made of wood or metal. The Ka-13 (foreground) has a welded steel tube fuselage and wood wings.

The advantage of a high aspect ratio wing is that it produces less drag than a short, broad wing. The light aeroplane pilot is prepared to accept a higher drag aircraft for the convenience of short wings for taxiing and hangarage, lower construction costs, and because he has an engine to pull him along. It is also cheaper to increase engine power than to reduce drag to any appre-

Above Sailplanes have long, narrow wings. This ASW-22 has a span of 24 metres.

Opposite The seagull's ratio of span to wing width (aspect ratio) is only 10.

Below Glass and carbon fibres make such long unsupported wings both strong and stiff enough.

ciable extent. The sailplane pilot—and designer—do not think this way. They are purists who search for perfection. But to soar high in the summer skies even better than the birds, the pilot is prepared to accept what becomes, on the ground, an inconvenient and easily damaged—though still beautiful—piece of hardware.

How a sailplane flies

A sailplane flies through the air in the same way as any other fixed-wing aircraft, in that the wing has to move fast enough to create enough lift to support the weight of the aircraft. To stay in the air it must have sufficient *airspeed*. To obtain the lift the wing has to meet the airflow at an angle which causes the air to flow efficiently over it: this is called the *angle of attack*. On a sailplane the angle of attack for normal flying is about 3°. If, when taking off, the nose is held down so that the angle of attack is less, the sailplane will not get into the air. If the angle of attack is increased to about 12°, the air flowing over the wing will no longer be able to do so smoothly. The wing will cease to be able to provide enough lift to continue to support the aircraft, and it will stall.

When the sailplane is being flown straight, the angle of attack is directly related to the indicated airspeed. When the nose is raised the angle of attack is increased and the airspeed indicator will show less speed. If it is lowered, the angle of attack is reduced and a greater airspeed is indicated. But this is only true for straight flight. In turns, particularly

steep turns, or when pulling out of a dive, there is an extra load on the wings, and the stalling angle will be reached at a higher airspeed. This is one of the important lessons in learning to fly.

The angle of attack, at which the wing meets the airflow in flight, is not the same as the *angle of incidence*, often called rigging incidence. This is the angle at which the wing is fixed to the fuselage. The designer has to compromise between setting this angle so that when the wing is being flown fast the fuselage will still present a low drag shape to the airflow, and relating the wing to the fuselage and its landing wheel to facilitate taking off and landing.

Unlike the aeroplane, which has an engine to provide the speed to fly, the sailplane obtains its airspeed from gravity. All the time it is airborne it is gliding down through the air; and it still continues to glide down when flying in an upcurrent. It gains height only because it is being carried bodily upwards by the rising mass of air. Since the pilot may not always find air that is going up when he needs it, he wants his sailplane to return to earth slowly, with as flat an angle of glide as possible. This is why designers are pestered by pilots for better and better performance.

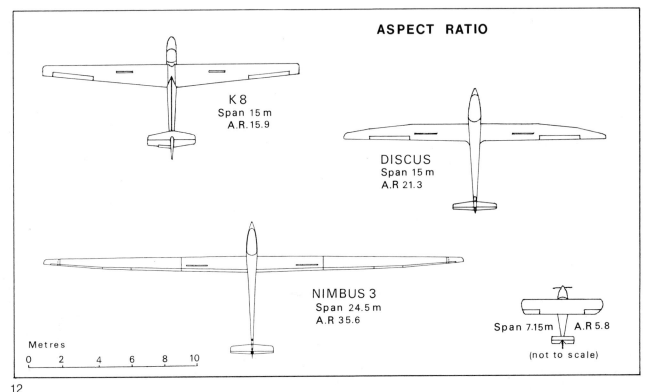

ASPECT RATIO

K 8
Span 15 m
A.R. 15.9

DISCUS
Span 15 m
A.R 21.3

NIMBUS 3
Span 24.5 m
A.R 35.6

Span 7.15m   A.R 5.8
(not to scale)

Metres
0   2   4   6   8   10

How performance is measured

The performance of a sailplane is measured in glide ratio and sink rate. Glide ratio is the distance a sailplane will travel per unit of height lost. For example: an ordinary production sailplane having a glide ratio of 45:1 would fly 45 miles from a height of 1 mile (5280 ft), or in metric units, 45 kilometres from a height of 1 km. This is its theoretical still air performance, taking no account of inaccurate flying.

Sink rate is the rate at which the sailplane will sink back to earth if no upcurrents are encountered. Our example sailplane above would have a sink rate of 135 ft/min (0.7m/sec). The airspeed at which the sailplane will achieve its minimum sink rate is just a little slower than the speed at which it has the flattest glide.

The sailplane pilot uses his airspeed in quite a different way from the aeroplane pilot, who prefers it to remain as constant as possible. The sailplane pilot wants to fly slowly in thermals, and at a low sink rate in weak conditions. He will then have more time to find upcurrents before subsiding on to the ground. But when thermals are strong, he wants to be able to fly between them at high speeds at a flat angle of glide. He wants the best of both worlds, and designers have become remarkably good at providing it.

Regardless of how strong the lift—or how jubilant the pilot may feel—there is a design limit to the speed at which a sailplane, or any aircraft,
should be flown. This maximum permitted speed, never exceed speed (Vne), or redline speed, is the maximum allowed speed for the structural strength of the aircraft. It is a compromise between speed, strength, and weight. The maximum permitted speed for smooth air for many high performance sailplanes is around 125 knots, but the rough air maximum speed is often much lower, around 80 knots. These speeds are placarded in the cockpit.

Drag

Drag is the resistance of the air to the passage of an object moving through it. You can feel it when you try to stand against a strong wind. The more streamlined the shape of the object, therefore, the more easily it will slip through the air.

Drag on an aircraft is of two sorts: *profile drag* and *induced drag*. The profile drag of a clean sailplane, undercarriage up, is mainly due to skin friction. On older gliders, most aeroplanes and hang gliders with the pilot in the open, profile drag is greater because the air cannot flow smoothly around the many obstructions and they produce turbulent wakes. Profile drag, as would be expected, worsens as speed is increased; so as the pilot in his clean, and slippery, ship flies fast between thermals, he must allow for some deterioration in his glide performance.

Induced drag is different. It is the drag produced by the wing in creating the lift it needs to fly. The lift
produced by the wing is an upward force applied to the wing by the passing airstream. The wing also exerts a force on the air, which is pushed downwards. This downward velocity represents wasted energy that is equivalent to a drag force, and leads to the generation of vortices, mainly from the wingtips. Such vortices from the wingtips of big jets, known as wake turbulence, are a notorious hazard to small aircraft flying up to several miles behind them.

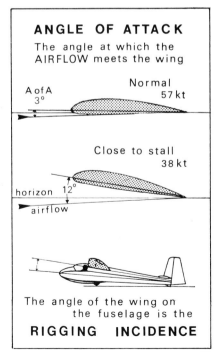

ANGLE OF ATTACK
The angle at which the AIRFLOW meets the wing

A of A 3° — Normal 57 kt

Close to stall 38 kt

horizon 12° — airflow

The angle of the wing on the fuselage is the
RIGGING INCIDENCE

Winglets on an ASW-20 to help reduce induced drag.

Although, the induced drag vortices are comparatively small on a well designed sailplane, they cannot be eliminated—otherwise the wing would not produce lift. Much research goes on to try to minimise induced drag, including adding winglets, giving the wing leading edge sweepback, or making the tips very small, but all attempts carry some price. Winglets may reduce induced drag, but they add to profile drag at higher speeds, and tiny wingtips may adversely affect stall behaviour. The problem is that with sailplane performance as high as it

already is, it is both difficult, and often very expensive, to make even a minute improvement.

To obtain the best performance from his sailplane the pilot needs to have some understanding of drag forces, because although profile drag increases the faster he flies, induced drag lessens, and it is worst at low speeds. Because of this there is a speed for each sailplane type at which the best compromise is obtained—where the induced and profile drags are equal. This speed gives the best angle of glide; it is the speed at which the sailplane will

The little winglets of the Discus are overshadowed by the wing's superb surface.

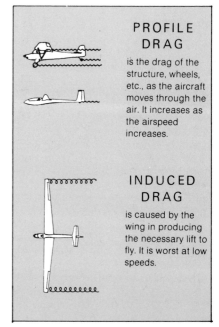

PROFILE DRAG

is the drag of the structure, wheels, etc., as the aircraft moves through the air. It increases as the airspeed increases.

INDUCED DRAG

is caused by the wing in producing the necessary lift to fly. It is worst at low speeds.

travel furthest from a given height in still air.

L/D or Lift over Drag
Sometimes the glide ratio is referred to as the L/D. This is because the

Flaps extended on a metal Blanik two-seater.

glide ratio is numerically equal to it: in straight flight the lift provided by the wing is equal to the weight of the aircraft. For example, the drag on a sailplane, such as the Discus, which weighs 500 kg (1100 lb), loaded, has a glide ratio of 41 at, say, 50 knots. Its L/D ratio at this speed is also 41, so its

actual drag is therefore only 500/41 = 12 kg (27 lb).

Laminar flow
As the airflow moves over the wing the particles of air closest to the surface will be slowed down. This creates skin friction drag, so the

designer goes to great trouble to ensure that the airflow is as smooth and as laminar as possible. The decelerated air forms a region known as the boundary layer. On a good, smooth wing the laminar flow will be about 1mm thick near the leading edge, to perhaps 5mm thick further back on the wing. Further back still the laminar flow becomes upset and the boundary layer air eddies instead of flowing smoothly. This is known as the laminar transition point. The turbulent eddies increase the thickness of the boundary layer, so that at the trailing edge of the wing it may be 25mm in thickness. This increases the drag per unit area more than 5 times.

The designer chooses a wing section which will have the laminar transition point as far back on the wing surface as he can get and the manufacturing processes will allow. But any roughness, paint lines or other surface discontinuities will result in the transition point moving forwards so that a higher proportion of the wing suffers from the faster moving turbulent air particles, with consequent degradation of the performance.

Some laminar flow wings are highly sensitive to raindrops, including water ballast dropped from another sailplane. This not only affects the performance but may also have a detrimental effect on the stall and slow speed behaviour.

Sailplane construction

Most sailplanes, other than school gliders, are made from glass fibre and epoxy resin. With this material it is much easier to build long, and strong, unsupported wings than it was in the past with wood, or even metal. Carbon fibres are usually included in the manufacturing process to make the long wings stiffer in bending and less floppy. No wing, however, should be too rigid or it would have to be made even stronger, and thus heavier, to absorb any severe turbulence to which it might be subjected.

Glass fibre is not only an excellent construction material from which to make big-span high aspect ratio wings; the whole sailplane can also be moulded to a highly efficient shape with a superbly smooth finish. It is so good that competition pilots will keep their wing covers on until just before take off to avoid the surface being roughened by dust or flies! Glass-fibre sailplanes are almost universally white because this keeps them cooler in hot sunshine than if they were coloured. Increasingly, though, they are given coloured noses, tails, or wing tips for better identification, and so that they will be more visible against a pale sky.

Many school gliders are still made from wood or metal—often having wooden wings and a welded steel tube fuselage. The learner pilot does not need high speed or superb performance while acquiring the flying basics; in fact, he will learn more quickly on a lower performance

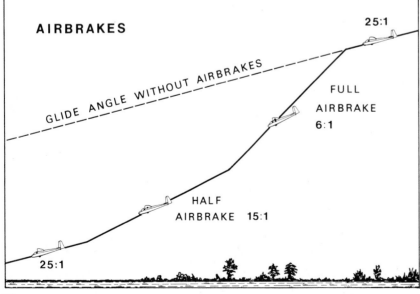

AIRBRAKES

25:1

GLIDE ANGLE WITHOUT AIRBRAKES

FULL AIRBRAKE 6:1

HALF AIRBRAKE 15:1

25:1

glider. School aircraft also have a hard working life and need to be easy to maintain and quick to repair.

Airbrakes

Just as the designer has created such a clean, slippery, high-speed sailplane, he has also created the very characteristics which make it difficult to get back on the ground again; even a large airfield would not be big enough to land a sailplane easily whose glide angle could not be reduced below, say, 50:1. So sailplanes are fitted with airbrakes, sometimes called dive breaks, which project from the wings. When these are opened into the airflow they in-crease the sailplane's profile drag enormously, which means that it has to be flown at a much steeper glide angle to maintain the same airspeed. The pilot can adjust the amount of airbrake surface that he presents to the airflow to achieve the glide path he needs to touch down on his chosen spot. Airbrakes produce only drag, and do not noticeably affect the stall speed.

Flaps

Flaps are different. Fitted to the trailing edges of the sailplane's wings inboard of the ailerons, they are used to alter the wing shape to give it a slower speed, higher-lift profile when lowered, or one more suited to high speed flying when they are raised above neutral. If the flaps are arranged so that they can be lowered to an angle approaching 90°, as they are on many aeroplanes, they will additionally increase drag and steepen the glide path in the same way as do airbrakes. If the sailplane is fitted with both flaps and airbrakes the pilot, when approaching to land, will firstly lower the flaps a little so that the wings continue to provide the necessary lift at a lower airspeed. He will then use the airbrakes to obtain his desired steeper glide path. A second-

Dumping water ballast at the end of a race.

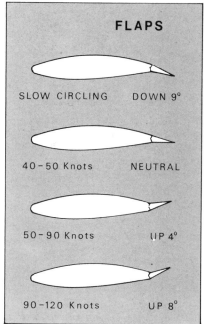

FLAPS

SLOW CIRCLING   DOWN 9°

40 - 50 Knots   NEUTRAL

50 - 90 Knots   UP 4°

90 - 120 Knots   UP 8°

ary advantage of the use of flaps, and/or airbrakes, is that the nose of the sailplane becomes lower than

Nimbus 3 pulling up after crossing the finish line.

normal so the pilot has a better view of the landing area ahead.

The main reason for fitting flaps on sailplanes is not for landing, but to improve the performance range

when soaring. When circling in a thermal, or endeavouring to stay airborne in weak conditions, lowering a small amount of flap will, as stated above, make the wing more efficient

at a lower airspeed. This means that the speed for minimum sink will also be lower. The pilot will be able to circle more slowly making smaller circles, and so will find it easier to stay in the stronger core of the thermal and to climb quickly. When he leaves the thermal and flies straight, without any lift or in sinking air, he wants to fly faster. He now raises the flaps to their neutral position, or if he wants to fly faster still, to a position slightly above neutral: this changes the wing profile to a higher speed section. The stall speed will now be higher, but this is unimportant as the pilot is intending only to use the fast end of his speed range. Using flaps so that the sailplane is always in the most efficient configuration for the conditions is a key skill for the soaring pilot to develop.

Weight

The weight at which a sailplane is flown affects both its stall speed and its performance at higher speeds. This is because weight affects the *wing loading*: this is the airborne weight of the sailplane divided by its wing area. If the sailplane is being flown by a heavy pilot, the higher wing loading will result in a slight increase in stall speed. With a light pilot the wing loading and the stall speed will both be lower.

The school glider on which the new pilot will build up his early solo flying hours weighs about 208 kg (458 lb) empty, and may be flown with a cockpit load (pilot, parachute, camera, etc.) ranging between 104 kg (229 lbs) and 57 kg (125 lb). The

wing loading will vary between 22 kg/m² (4.5 lb/ft²) and 18.7 kg/m² (3.8 lb/ft²).

The wing loading also affects the sailplane's performance at higher speeds, because at a higher wing loading it will be able to fly faster for the same glide performance than when the wing is more lightly loaded. The minimum sink rate will, of course, be higher with a heavy pilot than with a light one but, again, this is not important when the pilot is using the higher end of his speed range to fly fast between good thermals. If on a day of such thermals the pilot wants to be able to fly really fast, he will carry ballast to increase the wing loading still further. On glass-fibre sailplanes this is carried in the form of water in the wings. The maximum quantity of water which can be carried is given in the sailplane's certificate of airworthiness. Most glass-fibre sailplanes in general use can carry some 120 kg (265 lbs) of water ballast, although the capacity of a Nimbus 3 is 220 kg (485 lb). This raises the airspeed for best glide ratio (57:1) from 44 knots without ballast to the best L/D with ballast (the same, 57:1) at 53 knots.

You do not, of course, ever get something for nothing, and in addition to the expected higher stall speed (in the case of a fully loaded Nimbus 3 from 62 km/h (34 knots) to 75 km/h (41 knots)) such heavy sailplanes need a much more powerful tug to tow them into the air, have a longer take-off run, and have an appreciably higher landing speed.

When thermals weaken, either

because the weather deteriorates or it is late in the day, the pilot will dump some or all of his water ballast. Now he will again be flying at a lower wing loading, and be able to use the lower, slower end of his speed range more efficiently. Before landing he dumps all water ballast to reduce the landing speed.

Centre of gravity (or c.g.)

One important consideration concerning the weight of a sailplane is that the weight of the pilot, his equipment, and any ballast, shall be carried in such a way that the centre of gravity of the sailplane remains within the limits set by the designer. c.g. is expressed as the percentage of the mean chord of the wing, typically from 20%–36%, or from 25cm to 40cm aft of the leading edge. In a light aeroplane the pilot(s) usually sits under or above the wing close to the c.g., but in a sailplane the pilot is in front of the wing, and his weight may put the c.g. outside the limits. These limits *must* be observed, and if the pilot is so light that the minimum weight is not achieved, ballast to make up the weight must be carried in the cockpit. This usually takes the form of lead sheet or shot bags.

The trimmer

A sailplane is designed to be stable so that if the pilot flies 'hands off', without pushing or pulling on the stick, the aircraft will continue to fly steadily at a particular speed. However, the pilot may wish to fly faster or slower than this speed and he may be heavy or light in weight, so he needs some means of adjusting the trim speed to cope with a wide range of conditions.

Although it can be tiring to have to push continually on the stick to fly fast, or pull on it to fly slowly, the forces and movements to do this are in fact quite small. For example, a push (or pull) on the stick of, say, 1 kg will increase (or decrease) the speed by about 10 knots, while the stick movement is only 10mm or so. Nevertheless, on a long flight it is enough to be tedious. This is why it is desirable to have a trimmer.

The simplest trim control is a spring connecting the trim lever and the elevator control. By moving the lever the force applied to the elevator circuit can be varied. An alternative is to have a small tab built in to the trailing edge of the elevator. Movement of this tab by the trim lever results in an aerodynamic force being applied to the elevator. The K–8 is fitted with a trim tab. If the pilot wants to trim the aircraft to fly at a faster speed, he moves the trim lever *forwards*. This moves the tab on the elevator *up* into the airflow, causing a downward pressure on the elevator itself, and hence an increase in airspeed.

This section has looked at the sailplane itself. Parts 2 and 3 will refer to many of these aspects again from the pilot's point of view.

Effect of sailplane weight on its performance

Nimbus 3	Without ballast	With 220 kg ballast
wing span	24.5 m (80.36 ft)	same
wing area	16.76 m² (180.3 ft²)	same
weight	483 kg (1062 lb)	703 kg (1546 lb)
wing loading	28.8 kg/m² (5.89 lb/ft²)	41.9 kg/m² (8.57 lb/ft²)
stall speed	62 km/h (34 kt)	75 km/h (41 kt)
minimum sink rate	*0.36 m/s (0.7 kt)	*0.43 m/s (0.84 kt)
speed for minimum sink	76 km/h (41 kt)	92 km/h (49 kt)
best glide ratio	57:1	57:1
speed for best glide	80 km/h (43 kt)	96 km/h (52 kt)
sink speed at 200 km/h	2.84 m/s (5.6 kt)	2.08 m/s (4.1kt)
glide ratio at 200 km/h	*19.4:1	*26.5:1

The effect of ballast is best shown by comparing the two sets of figures marked*. The minimum sink speed has increased by 19%, but the glide ratio at 200 km/h (108 kt) has gone up by 37%. Unless upcurrents are very weak, or small so that increased circling speed is a disadvantage, ballast will give a higher average cross-country speed.

The pilot's headrest is attached to the canopy. The hole in the nose contains the airspeed indicator pitot head.

✈ **Sailplane rigging and inspection**

Rigging

Sailplanes have trailers because they may land out on a cross-country flight and have to be retrieved. They are also used for normal storage,

with the aircraft being de-rigged at the end of each day's flying. Because of this frequent rigging, or dismantling, sailplanes are designed and constructed so that it is simple and quick to do, and, much more important, very difficult to do wrong. The designer, however, cannot prevent a pilot forgetting to connect up his elevator or ailerons, so the whole business of rigging is a serious one demanding both concentration and commonsense.

The wings, fuselage and tailplane are held in fittings in the trailer and are slid out on runners without any need to enter the trailer; in fact, some fit around the sailplane so closely that there is no room to do so. When

the fuselage, and afterwards the wings, are brought from the trailer they have to be temporarily held in supports until they are put together. These vary according to the pilot's system or circumstances, and some owners have so mechanised their rigging that they can do it alone. Most sailplanes, however, are rigged by two or three people, and on the morning of a good soaring day club pilots help to rig each other's machines.

There are two possible hazards when rigging—someone slips and drops a wing or tailplane, or the pilot fails to check that the rigging is correct and complete (this check should be done by the pilot because

Upper photograph Wings are heavy, especially when carrying them up hill.

Lower photograph It is easier to check everything with a helper holding the wings level.

Opposite Putting a Ka-6 together in Iceland can also be cold.

22

he is the one who is going to fly the aircraft). The risk of dropping a wing is obviously least when the person carrying or supporting it has done the job many times before, whereas it will be greatest when he does not know anything about gliding, or does not appreciate that a wing is heavy— or that a tailplane can be swept out of his hands by the wind. It is up to the pilot himself to brief such helpers carefully as to what they have to do.

Having assembled the sailplane the pilot must go round it and check that each connection has been properly made, and any pins are correctly secured. He should then double-check this by moving the stick and rudder in the cockpit to ensure that the ailerons, elevator, flaps, air-brakes, etc., move fully and freely in the *correct sense*. Only then should any fairings be attached and secured. This is the rigging check and it should be done as soon as the sailplane is assembled.

Daily inspection

The rigging check only ensures that the sailplane has been put together properly. It does not take account of accidental damage, wear or tear, or unserviceable instruments. These things are looked after by the next check—usually called the Daily Inspection (DI). This should be done before the first take off on every flying day, after every outlanding, and whenever the sailplane has been left unattended in a public place. Some pilots think that the inspection can be carried out at the launch point, but it is only sensible to do it near the

A typical club open trailer which can be persuaded to carry different types of glider.

hangar or trailer, where it is easier to undertake any work or polishing that needs to be done. Once at the launch point there is not only distraction in talking to other pilots, but also an inclination to put off minor jobs because of the inconvenience in taking the sailplane all the way back to the hangar. Most clubs insist that the sailplane's Daily Inspection book has been signed by the pilot before he arrives out on the field to fly.

The Daily Inspection is best done with a check list. The one on page 28 covers sailplanes in general, but the wise owner will make out a special

A competition sailplane will have its own close-fitting trailer.

Rigging a club two-seater. This Blanik arrived after being repaired on a spare trailer to be rigged by club members—some of them doing it for the first time. **A** Putting the canopy out of harm's way, on tyres to keep it off the ground. **B** Lifting off the right wing. **C** Undoing the lashing that had been needed to hold down the tail; note how the tailplane folds up against the rudder. **D** Taking off the left wing to lay it on more tyres. **E** Now for the fuselage; but as this temporary trailer has no front supports, two people sit on the rear end to hold it down. **F** Fuselage safely off.

G

G

H

I

J

G Greasing the main pins which attach the wings to the fuselage. **H** Now for the right wing. **I** The wing has to be held firmly and positioned carefully to line up the attachment fittings. **J** The two wingtip helpers must be careful not to exert too much leverage. By the time a newcomer has been in his gliding club for a year he will have become expert at rigging and dismantling sailplanes.

one that takes account of his own aircraft's peculiarities.

Like the rigging check the DI needs to be done systematically and thoroughly, starting at the cockpit and controls, and working right

Wings on ground handling wheels make shady places on a hot day.

round the aircraft and back again to the cockpit. But even with a check list the 'inspector' must consider the use to which the aircraft is put. If it is his own sailplane, and flown only by him, he will know how much flying he has done and how the aircraft has been handled. In this case he will need to

look most carefully to see if the sailplane has been damaged after being left in the hangar, and must look for anything different from normal. More searching should be the inspection of a well-used school two-seater. Not only will it be doing a lot of flying and be subjected to

plenty of wear and tear, but it will be no stranger to heavy landings; and all sorts of things from pencils to money will have been dropped in the cockpit and may find their way into the fuselage, possibly to jam the controls.

Being interrupted while inspecting a sailplane is the best way to forget something. If distracted, you should either start again from the beginning of the check list, or re-start at least one item *before* the one you were doing when interrupted.

Every sailplane should have its own inspection or log book, whether or not required by law, and it should be signed and dated every time an inspection is made. It should also include work done, such as a tyre changed or an instrument replaced. If nothing else, a log book may make it easier to sell your sailplane when you become starry-eyed about buying a new model.

Pre-flight check

There is a third pre-flight inspection—sometimes called a cockpit check. This is done prior to *every* take off, and since it is one of the fundamental lessons the new pilot must learn, it is dealt with in Part 2, Learning to fly.

Inspecting the trailer

For occasional retrieves of club gliders an open trailer which will carry different types is both cheap and convenient, but for the owner who uses his trailer as his sailplane's home it has to be really worthy of its contents. It is not too difficult to make

Top A fuselage support to help rigging with only two people.

Bottom This tough detachable tailwheel saves sailplane wear when towing out over rough ground.

Sailplane daily inspection check list

There is no special order in which an aircraft should be checked, and owners work out a system that suits them. The essential requirements are thoroughness and integrity—*not* noticing something wrong and hoping it will cure itself, or waiting for another day. The following list starts with the cockpit (and the controls) and ends at the cockpit. This time to check loose equipment.

COCKPIT *Check:*
    Airworthiness certificate valid, log book up-to-date, faults rectified.
    General cleanliness and condition of cockpit, seat, and harness.
    Controls: all moving fully and in the correct sense.
    Trimmer, flaps, and airbrakes as above.
    Undercarriage lever locked down.
    Release operating freely and release hook clean.
    Instruments working, including radio, batteries OK, altimeter set.
    Canopy undamaged and catches in good condition.

WINGS *Check:*
    For cracks, dents, holes, bruising.
    Wings correctly attached to fuselage and pins locked.
    Ailerons moving fully and correctly (double-check). Hinges OK.
    Airbrakes flush with wing surface when closed and locked.
    Flaps connected. Fairings in place and secured.

TAIL *Check:*
    For cracks, dents, holes, bruising.
    Tailplane and elevator correctly attached and locked.
    Elevator moving fully and correctly (double-check).
    Trim tab working. If fixed tab, at correct angle.
    Rudder moving fully (double-check).
    Tailskid or tail wheel in good condition.

FUSELAGE *Check:*
    For cracks, dents, holes, bruising.
    Main landing wheel and tyre in good condition. Tyre pressure correct.
    Undercarriage doors undamaged.

COCKPIT EQUIPMENT *Check:*
    Parachute in good condition. Repacking date not passed.
    Ballast (if needed) installed securely in cockpit.
    Barograph and turn point cameras installed and working.
    Water ballast tanks and taps serviceable.
    Maps to cover proposed route.

sure that it does not leak, and that the fittings will support the wings and fuselage in a way that will not cause them wear or strain, but the trailer's roadworthiness must be good as well. The two essentials are that the trailer is stable on tow; and this means slightly nose heavy and not tail heavy, and that it will not break free from the towing car. It can do this in three ways: the tow bar can come off the car, the tow bar cup can part company with the tow bar ball, or the trailer tow bar can break. If the car is bought with a tow bar already fitted, this should be carefully examined to see that welds are not cracked or bolts loose. Most countries have trailer towing regulations and, if taking a trailer to another country, it is worth finding out before you go any differences in requirements.

Some people seem to think that once the sailplane is in its trailer it will be safe, but it does not take a storm force wind to blow a trailer over. If leaving it on an airfield for any length of time, tie it down securely.

Club Libelle: span 15 m (49.2 ft), empty weight
180 kg (397 lb), glide ratio 33:1.

Parachutes

It is standard practice to wear a parachute when soaring, and all sailplane seats are designed to take them. Parachutes are not carried because sailplanes are structurally weak, but to save the pilot in the event of a collision. In thermals there are often large concentrations of sailplanes flying close to each other and the risk is obvious. Pilots, naturally, keep a good look out and fly in a disciplined manner, but mistakes can occur.

Parachutes are of use only when they are worn correctly and maintained in good condition. Should you ever need to jump in a hurry, it will not be the moment to remember that you have been using your life-saver as a seat cushion, or that it has not been repacked for years. Although parachutes are now made from tough synthetic fibres instead of the traditional silk, they will still be more reliable if kept dry and away from contaminating substances, such as oil or cleaning fluids.

Should the worst happen and part of the wing or the tail is broken in flight, the sailplane will not only become uncontrollable but may subject the pilot to high g forces. This may make it extremely difficult to get clear of the cockpit. No pilot may wish to think about such things, but it is in his interest to do so, and to work out how he would lever himself out of his seat—having remembered to first jettison the canopy and undo his harness! Thinking this problem through from time to time, as well as talking to any pilot who has ever used a parachute 'in anger', may just save those vital seconds should you ever have to jump.

30

Sailplane parachutes are back type but most are made very slim to fit slender glass-fibre cockpits.

The instrument panel may be built in to the
canopy or the cockpit.

Instruments

Sailplanes, like many light aeroplanes, can be flown safely without
instruments, but they are *essential* to
get the best from the aircraft's performance. The three most important are
the airspeed indicator (ASI), the altimeter, and the variometer. The ASI
gives the sailplane's speed through
the air, the altimeter presents an
indication of its height, and the
variometer shows the pilot whether
he is rising or sinking. The student
pilot will learn how to use these
instruments separately, and for him
the airspeed indicator is the most
useful, but for soaring the information from all three must be closely
interrelated. This is because the pilot
wants to fly at different airspeeds
according to whether thermals are
strong or weak. However, the most
important lessons to learn about instruments are that (a) they sometimes go wrong, and (b) the information presented should not be taken
at face value unless the pilot under-
stands exactly what the readings
mean.

The Airspeed Indicator (ASI)

The ASI gives the speed of the sailplane through the air (airspeed), or
put another way, the speed at which
the air is moving past the wing. It is
merely a sensitive pressure gauge
which measures the difference in air
pressure between that in a tube fac-
ing forwards into the airflow (the pitot
tube) and a sensing point in undis-
turbed air (the static). The pitot
tube—named after the eighteenth-
century French scientist Henri Pitot—
can be mounted on the wing or
fuselage, but on sailplanes it is usually seen as a hole in the extreme

31

nose which contains a tube connecting it to one side of the instrument. The static is connected to the other side. This can also be a tube, aligned with the airflow but blocked at the front, with tiny holes through its sides; or there may just be holes on both sides of the fuselage. The location of these fuselage holes is carefully chosen to provide neither pressure nor suction, and they are connected together, with a tube to the instrument running from this link. If this were not done errors in the ASI reading would occur whenever the sailplane was not being flown quite straight.

The sailplane ASI works mechanically, having a capsule or diaphragm which deflects under pressure. This deflection is magnified by levers and a gear train to drive the needle which moves around the dial. The pressure in the system is quite low, and since human lungs are powerful the instrument is likely to be damaged if the pitot is blown into to see if the ASI is working.

The ASI may be calibrated in knots, mph, or km/h, and this should be checked if the pilot is lent a sailplane in another country. If he is used to coming in to land at 50 knots and carelessly approaches at 50 km/h, he will be in for an unpleasant surprise.

The ASI only gives the sailplane's airspeed. It takes no account of the wind which is drifting the sailplane over the ground. When flying into wind the airspeed will be faster than the groundspeed. When flying cross-country downwind a windspeed of 20 knots will give a free distance bonus

of 20 miles for each hour's flying.

ASI errors Indicated airspeed (IAS) is what the instrument reads, but errors may occur due to the location of the static, and possibly the pitot. This is known as *pressure error*, and is normally quite small. For example, the ASI may under-read by 3 knots at the stall, and exaggerate by 4 knots at maximum permitted speed. The equivalent airspeed (EAS) is the IAS corrected for pressure error.

The calibration of an ASI is based on Standard Atmosphere density at sea level. If the air density in which the aircraft is flying is less than this, as when it is flying high, the actual airspeed will be higher than that shown on the instrument, but this is only of importance when taking off or landing, and for navigation. The stalling speed varies with density in exactly the same way, but the *indicated airspeed* (IAS) at the stall will always be the same regardless of the height. The true airspeed (TAS) is the equivalent airspeed (EAS) corrected for the density effect. For example, at 10,000 ft the TAS is 1.16 times the EAS.

The altimeter

The altimeter shows height, but like the ASI it may not always give the pilot the information he thinks he is getting. The instrument is basically a sealed pressure gauge with the dial or face calibrated in feet or metres on an arbitrary international standard. Air pressure at 1013.2 mb is taken as zero feet or metres, and reduced pressure represents various heights. For example, 506 mb is taken as

18,000 ft, or 5488 metres.

If the actual pressure at sea level happened to be 1013.2 mb and the temperature of the air at increasing heights was also 'standard', then the altimeter would read the height of the aircraft above sea level. However, the pressure at sea level is rarely precisely 1013.2 mb, so the datum point of the instrument is made adjustable by means of a knob near the bottom of the dial. When flying from an airfield at sea level, the altimeter can be adjusted to read exactly zero. If flying from a field on higher ground whose height above sea level is known, then this height can be set before take off. In both cases the altimeter will give height above sea level during the flight. Alternatively, the altimeter can be set to read zero on the elevated airfield, and during the flight it will show height above the airfield—or a lower height over lower ground.

As well as having an adjustment by reference to its height scale, most altimeters have a pressure scale calibrated in mb. This allows the altimeter to be set in the air, or on the ground, to the prevailing air pressure. For example, the pilot can call on the radio for the sea level setting (called QNH) or the airfield setting (QFE). If he sets QFE on his altimeter in the air and then lands at the airfield, his altimeter will read zero at touch down.

The problem with altimeters is that any setting is correct only at the time of making it because the air pressure at sea level is changing all the time. In the centre of an anticyclone pressure

may rise to 1040 mb, and in a deep depression may fall to perhaps 960 mb. In such an extreme case the pressure difference of 80 mb corresponds to a height difference of 2900 ft or 880 metres! In practice, when flying towards an area of lowering pressure the altimeter will over-read, showing the pilot height that he does not have. The opposite applies when flying towards high pressure. To the sailplane pilot such errors are of less importance than to an aeroplane pilot who may be flying in weather poor enough to keep sailplanes on the ground. What is important to the soaring pilot is that he must remember that his altimeter will not tell him how high he is above the fields below him, and in which he may have to land. This is why, when learning to fly, it is necessary to develop a good visual judgement of the sailplane's height above the ground.

The ordinary altimeter is a reasonably robust instrument, remaining fairly accurate after years of use, but because of the lack of vibration on a sailplane the needle may stick—a light tap on the instrument panel should be enough to get it moving. Usually the altimeter casing is connected to the airspeed indicator static vent, but if the static connection is left open to the cockpit, errors can occur when flying fast.

Variometer

The word variometer is used in connection with sailplanes and balloons, but rate of climb, or vertical speed indicator (VSI), with aeroplanes. The variometer is the fundamental instru-

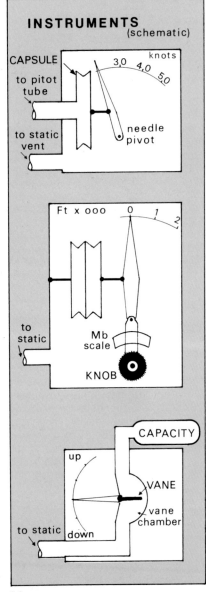

INSTRUMENTS
(schematic)

CAPSULE

knots

3,0 4,0 5,0

to pitot tube

to static vent

needle pivot

Ft x ooo 0 1 2

to static

Mb scale

KNOB

CAPACITY

up

VANE

vane chamber

to static down

AIRSPEED INDICATOR

Increase of pressure inside the capsule causes it to expand and move the needle.

The ASI shows the speed of the aircraft through the air: the airspeed.

ALTIMETER

The capsule expands when pressure drops inside the instrument case, and moves the needle.

The adjustment knob enables the pilot to set the altimeter to read above sea level, or airfield height. In flight the altimeter can be adjusted for correct millibar setting by radio.

VARIOMETER

The vane in the chamber is centralised by a hair spring, and connected to the needle by a shaft on its pivot. If the sailplane climbs, the air pressure at the static will decrease. The air in the capacity will flow through the vane chamber and along the static tube. In doing so it deflects the vane and the needle shows the rate of climb.

ment for soaring, and enables up-currents to be detected and the best area to be located much more effectively than with an altimeter, or by 'feel'.

Until recently variometers worked on the basis of measuring the rate of flow of air out of, or into, a container. This could be the instrument casing, but was more usually a vacuum flask, called the capacity. Mechanically this can be done by a restriction in the capacity tube and measuring the pressure drop across this restriction. This type is common on aeroplanes but for sailplanes is too slow to respond. Another simple alternative is to use two coloured pistons in slightly tapered tubes. The pistons, or pellets, green for up and red for down, are moved by the air flowing in or out of the capacity. The most common mechanical varios use a small vane inside an annular chamber, with movement of the air into or out of the capacity causing the vane to deflect. This moves the instrument needle.

Some variometers are calibrated in hundreds of feet per minute and some in knots (1 knot = approximately 100 ft/min). This is a useful calibration as it enables the pilot to relate easily his airspeed, rate of sink and glide ratio. For example, if airspeed is 60 knots and the rate of sink is 2 knots, the actual glide ratio being achieved is 30:1 (assuming no wind).

Metric variometers are calibrated in metres a second which makes mental comparison more difficult.
Electric variometers Measuring the flow through the instrument can be

done electrically by two thermisters in the air pipe, the thermisters being heated electrically. When the air flows the thermister temperatures alter, resulting in changes of electrical resistance which can be translated into vertical speed. A newer type has an extremely sensitive pressure

A good compass is necessary when soaring over this type of empty country.

transducer measuring the local air pressure. The rate of change of this pressure is shown as vertical speed.

One great advantage of the electrical variometer is that it is simple to incorporate an audible signal. A change of pitch (or frequency of pulse) indicates rise or sink with the appropriate rate. The audio vario frees the pilot from constant obser-

vation of the instrument so that he can keep a good look out for other aircraft.

Whatever type of variometer is used the instrument has to be connected to the outside air. On simple installations this is the same static as for the ASI and altimeter, but it produces a somewhat disconcerting characteristic. Even in calm air minor

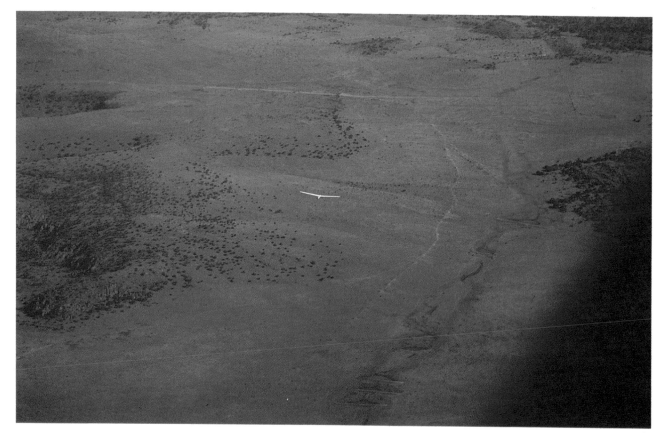

variations in airspeed result in changes in the vario readings. For example, decreasing speed from 50 to 45 knots puts the sailplane about

The variometer. Some are calibrated in metres per second, others in hundreds of feet per minute, or knots. 1 knot is approximately 100ft/min.

21 feet higher than it would have been if it had continued at the higher speed. If such a change of speed were spread over 3 seconds, the simple vario would incorrectly show a climb increment of 7 ft/sec, or 4 knots, for this period. For the pilot it is difficult to distinguish between a real upcurrent, and the 'stick thermal' caused by decreasing his airspeed. The problem can be overcome by making the instrument show rate of change of *total energy* (height with airspeed compensation), instead of only rate of change of height. On a perfect installation in calm air the total energy vario would show the rate of sink corresponding to the instantaneous speed at which the sailplane was flying, regardless of any rapid changes of airspeed. There are various ways of achieving total energy indications: the most common is to connect the instrument to a source of suction whose value is equal to the pressure in the pitot head, instead of to the usual static. This suction (reduced pressure) can be obtained by a small venturi, or by the Irving tube, which is a pipe having holes on its rear side. This is usually mounted, pointing forwards, from the leading edge of the fin.

The compass

On a sailplane the compass is not the primary navigational instrument. This is the pilot's eyes and his ability to use a map. The compass is used

The Cambridge Navigation Director provides the pilot with computerised assistance on the best speed to fly and final glide calculations.

more as a guide for setting off in the right direction after circling in lift, or for coming out of cloud. Nevertheless, any compass fitted in a sailplane should be a good one, and the pilot should understand the errors to which it is subject.

Magnetic variation is the difference between North as shown on the compass (magnetic North) and North as shown on the map (True North). Variation varies, and at present (1986) in Britain is 7° West. This means that if the pilot wants to fly due North (360°) on the map, he must fly with his compass reading 007°. If he wants to fly SW (225°) on the map, his compass must read 232°. (In Sydney, Australia, variation is currently 15°W and in Winnipeg 10°E.)

Deviation is a quite different sort of compass error, and is caused by magnetic metals close to the instrument. This can be checked easily, and a deviation card made for the cockpit. The simplest way to check the deviation is to position the sailplane well clear of confusions, such as hangars clad in corrugated iron, and to stand directly behind it with a reliable hand-bearing or orienteering compass. Take a reading of the heading of the sailplane, note it, and compare it with the reading on the installed cockpit compass. Turn the sailplane in steps of, say, thirty degrees, until back on the original heading. Now plot the results. This work will, of course, be useless if the pilot then carries other magnetic influences, such as camera light-meters, near the compass.

The normal compass is ineffective

when an aircraft is turning or the airspeed is altering. Some compasses, such as the Bohli, Cook, and Schantz compasses, are gimballed so that they will give a better indication of heading when the aircraft is turning.

The watch

The humble watch is a valuable navigational instrument. On any cross-country attempt, take-off and release times should be noted, as well as the times at which prominent landmarks or turn points are reached. With this information it is not difficult to work out average speeds, or the effect of the wind.

Blind flying instruments

Cloud flying by sailplanes is prohibited in many countries, so there is little need to install turn and slip indicators or artificial horizons. If a pilot needs assurance that he is flying his sailplane accurately, it is cheap to fit a small curved tube containing a ball, or even more simple to tape a short length of wool or thread in front of the canopy. If, however, cloud flying is permitted, and the pilot wants to acquire the skill to do it properly, he should equip himself with the best instrument that he can afford.

The *artificial horizon* is best. This presents a gyroscopically stabilized horizon behind a fixed aircraft symbol on the instrument face. If the horizon tips over to the left, for example, this shows that the sailplane is banked and turning to the right.

The turn-and-slip indicator is also gyroscopically controlled, but only in one plane: yaw. It is simpler and cheaper, but demands more interpretation and concentration.

Radio

Most sailplanes used for cross-country flying or competitions have radio, primarily for communication with the contest organisers and for giving progress reports and information to the crew about outlandings. Should cloud flying be permitted, pilots can inform others as to where and when they entered cloud, and height changes as they climb inside.

In the UK radio installations in both sailplane and retrieve car have to be of approved types and must be licensed. The British Gliding Association has four allotted frequencies: 129.9 MHz (ground to ground), 130.1, usually for competitions, 130.25 for general use, and 130.4 for cloud flying. Provided that radio is used only on these frequencies the pilot and car driver do not need operators' licences. If, however, the glider is equipped with a radio having frequencies used by Air Traffic Control, the pilot must have a personal radio licence in the same way as any aeroplane pilot.

It is a requirement of aircraft radios that the accuracy of the tuning is precise at a separation of only 0.25 MHz. A full 720 channel radio is expensive, but fits in the instrument panel and weighs less than 1 kg. To avoid the aerodynamic drag of an external aerial, it is built into the fin of glass-fibre sailplanes.

Theoretically VHF radio range is 'line of sight', which means that when soaring over fairly flat country at 2000 ft or so air-to-ground conversations are clear up to 30 miles, with air-to-air up to at least 60 miles (100 km) and frequently much further.

The aviation emergency frequency is 121.5 MHz.

The barograph

For records, contests, and for Silver, Gold, and Diamond Badge flights the sailplane has to carry a barograph. This is used to record the height which the pilot achieved, and also to show that the flight was made without an intermediate landing. Most aviation barographs are smaller versions of the traditional house barograph, but they indicate height instead of pressure. The height scale usually goes to 20,000 ft, with the drum rotating one revolution in 4, 8, or 12 hours. Ink is rarely used to mark the chart as it is messy and inclined to freeze. Normally, the drum is wrapped in paper or aluminium foil which is smoked with a sooty flame. The stylus is a sharp point which traces a very fine line. After landing the smoked paper is fixed with a setting fluid, such as an alcohol/shellac solution. Other types of barograph use waxed paper with an electrically heated stylus, or a mechanism to prick the recording paper with the stylus every few seconds.

Before flight the barograph has to be sealed by an Official Observer. After landing the pilot gives the barograph, still sealed, to the Observer, who will open it, sign the chart, and see that it is fixed.

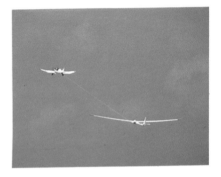

Launching methods

There are several methods of launching sailplanes into the air, each with special advantages. They are aerotowing, winch launching, car towing, and bungie (rubber catapult) launching.

Aerotowing

Aerotowing is the most versatile and popular among soaring pilots because the launch can start from any airfield or large field, and the aeroplane can tow the glider to an area and height where good thermals can be found. The sailplane is positioned on the ground behind a light aeroplane which is fitted with a tow hook and release in the region of its tailwheel, and the two are linked by a synthetic fibre tow rope (this has a breaking load of around 500 kg (1100 lb)), or a stronger rope with a weak link. At a given signal the aeroplane moves forwards to tighten the rope, then takes off and climbs to a height—usually about 600–700m (2000 ft)—where the sailplane pilot releases his end of the rope and flies free. The tow plane dives back to earth, lands, and tows up the next waiting sailplane.

The tug, often a Pawnee, Super Cub, Rallye or Cessna, is powered by an engine of 120–180 hp, although engines of 200 hp or more are needed to tow off big competition sailplanes when they are full of water ballast. To keep down the cost of tows the tug needs to climb at 500 ft/min (2.5 m/sec) or better, otherwise the turn round is uneconomically slow. A good tug pilot can give about 6 tows an hour.

The length of tow ropes varies from about 20 m (66ft) to 60 m (200 ft). At each end of the rope there is a pair of linked rings. Normally, the smaller of the two is put into the release hooks of the tug and of the sailplane.

In most countries the sailplane is towed in the high tow position, so that it flies just above the tug's slipstream. Low tow, with the sailplane just below the slipstream is also used,

Low tow position, with the sailplane below the slipstream.

mainly in Australia. It is more stable, and the risk of the glider getting too high and causing the tow plane to dive does not exist; but should the rope break there is more risk of it

On tow behind a Wilga tug. This tow rope is short. It is easier to tow with a rope about 50 metres long.

A club winch. If the ground is rough or soft a tractor is used to pull out the cable to the launch point.

flicking back over the sailplane and fouling the control surfaces. When low tow is used the pilot should move up into the high tow position before releasing, otherwise the tug pilot cannot see if the sailplane is free of the rope.

Winch launching

A winch launch is less expensive than an aerotow, and has the advantage that it can take place over rough ground which would be impossible for taking off in an aeroplane. It is, however, more limited in its scope and the height that it can provide. The winch itself is a stationary vehicle—and so it may have to be towed out to the upwind end of the airfield before launching can commence. It has a powerful engine of some 200 hp, which is connected to a drum holding about 1000 m (3280 ft) of stranded steel cable. This has a breaking load of some 1000 kg (2200 lb), and a weak link at the sailplane end. It has to be tough cable because it is subjected to heavy wear when being dragged along the ground to the sailplane, and then dropped back on to it after the launch. Near the end of the cable there is a small parachute, which remains closed during the launch and opens as the cable falls free to prevent it falling in a

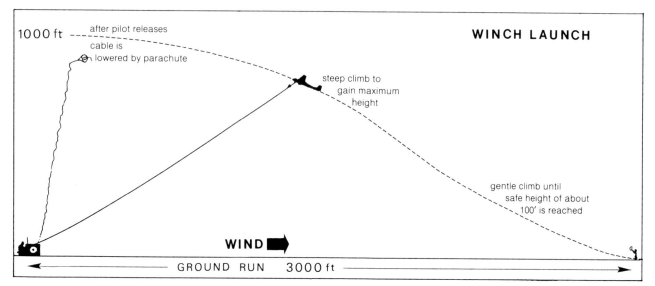

1000 ft — — — — —
after pilot releases
cable is
lowered by parachute

WINCH LAUNCH

steep climb to
gain maximum
height

gentle climb until
safe height of about
100' is reached

WIND ➡

GROUND RUN   3000 ft

tangled heap. This parachute also makes the end of the cable clearly visible to the winch driver, so that in rain or poor visibility he can see when the cable is being released. This could be vital because, in the rare event of the release jamming, the winch driver must immediately sever the cable at his end. The sailplane pilot will still be left with a length of trailing wire, but this is not as dangerous as being attached like a fish on a line.

The release mechanism is usually guarded by a ring against which the cable would bear if the sailplane overflew the winch. A load on this back releasing ring overcomes a spring to allow the cable to disengage from the hook.

The winch launch starts in the same way as an aerotow, with the winch driver on receipt of the 'take up slack' signal slowly pulling in the cable until it is taut. When the 'all out' signal is given, he winds in the cable fast enough to give the sailplane flying speed so that it will take off and climb. When the sailplane can get no more height, because the cable is now beginning to exert a downward pull, the pilot releases. An efficient winch can launch about 8 sailplanes an hour to 1000 ft or so, if the ground over which the cable has to be retrieved is relatively flat and smooth.

Many winches have two drums to help speed up the launch rate. Both cables are pulled out together, but if

there is any cross wind the downwind cable must be used first, so that it will fall clear of the windward one.

Car towing

Car towing is very similar to winching, but is simpler and quicker, provided a smooth runway of 1000 m (3280 ft) or more is available. Piano wire is used instead of stranded cable as it is more resistant to being dragged along concrete runways, but it kinks and breaks if bent too much. The wire is laid out straight along the runway, with one end attached to the tow car. This needs automatic transmission and an engine of some 180 hp; and it should be cut down behind the cab so that the driver can observe the

launch. The sailplane is attached and the signals and procedures are as for a winch launch. When the car approaches the end of the runway the driver slows and stops, and the sailplane pilot, feeling the deceleration, releases. When the wire reaches the ground the car driver releases his end of it, picks up the sailplane end, and tows it quickly back to the launch point. A single tow car and wire can provide around 10 launches an hour.

Clubs try to make their launching efficient to avoid long queues of waiting pilots, but often it is the pilots themselves who cause delays by not being ready when their turn comes. If each pilot at a busy launch point is

Release hook fitting on the tailskid of a Wilga tug for aerotowing.

late by only one minute this can mean that some 15 launches will be lost by the end of the day—which is most frustrating for the fifteen pilots robbed of their opportunity to take off.

Bungie launching

This was once the most popular way of launching, when light gliders flew from hills as hang gliders do today. Bungie launching is practised only rarely now because sailplanes have become heavy and fast—and because other ways of launching are readily available from flat ground. It is, however, a cheap way of getting into the air because all that is needed is a rubber rope and a good supply of enthusiastic helpers.

Sailplanes, such as the K–8 and some slow two-seaters with plenty of wing area, can be bungied provided they have a suitable release hook. In past years gliders were launched on an open hook, from which the rubber catapult simply fell when its energy had been expended. More recently the normal, closed release hooks have been used, which would back-release automatically as soon as the sailplane passed the point at which the bungie would have fallen off. This was essential in case the pilot forgot to release, or was late in doing so.

To launch, the sailplane is faced into wind on the hill top, held down in strong winds to avoid it being blown over, and the bungie is hooked on.

The launch crew, usually 4–5 a side, position themselves down the face of the slope with the rubber rope taut. Another helper lies on the ground holding on to the tailskid. The pilot shouts 'Walk!', and the bungie crew starts stretching the rope. When he shouts 'Run!' the crew run hard down the slope, trying not to fall over stones or tussocks. And when the bungie is fully extended, he calls 'Let go!' At this the helper hanging on to the tail does so—unless the sailplane has already been pulled out of his hands! The sailplane shoots into the air, and the pilot immediately turns along the hill to soar in its upcurrents (see page 80, Hill soaring).

Bungie ropes are made from bound filaments of rubber, usually 16 mm ($\frac{5}{8}$ inch) in diameter, have rope extensions for the pulling crew, and are fitted with a suitable ring or rings at the sailplane end.

The hill top should be smooth and rounded so that there is no risk of the crew falling over the edge, or the sailplane doing the same before it has flying speed.

In the early days of gliding, when most gliders were strut-braced, it was possible to launch them in fresh winds without any bungie at all. The

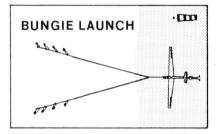

A vintage Olympia launched by bungie from a hill top.

glider was lifted off the ground, almost at flying speed in the strong wind, by a helper under each wing holding the top of the wing struts. As soon as a gust arrived the pilot shouted 'Launch!', and the helpers literally threw the glider into the air.

Bungie launching can get 15 or more gliders into the air in an hour, provided the helpers do not collapse exhausted.

Releases

Very good release mechanisms on both the sailplane and towing vehicle are essential if launching is to be safe. They must not only be hard-wearing, but have reliable automatic release capability. Just as important, they must be easy to inspect and remove for repair, and must be positioned so that they do not become clogged with mud or freezing snow. Some releases do not meet all these requirements as well as they should. On some glass-fibre sailplanes they are difficult to remove, and some do not open readily when the cable pull becomes badly offset. On many sail-planes, where every effort has been made to reduce drag, the mechanism is installed in the hole into which the landing wheel is retracted. This re-quires the pilot to remember not to lift his undercarriage until after he has released! The nearness of the release hook to the landing wheel also means that should the sailplane slightly over-run the cable at the start

of a launch there is a chance that it could get caught behind the wheel. If the sailplane runs forwards slightly and then stops, the pilot must im-mediately pull his release knob, and shout 'Stop!' to the signaller.

When buying a second-hand sailplane special attention should be given to the condition and position of the release hook. If it is near the nose of the sailplane it will be good for aerotowing, but not satisfactory for winch or car towing. For these methods it needs to be further back, nearer to the sailplane's centre of gravity so that it can climb steeply on the wire. On new sailplanes the hook is installed in a compromise position, but this is not always satisfactory. If it

is in a position more suited to winch launching, a light-weight or inexperi-enced pilot who gets too high while being aerotowed may find it difficult to return to the correct position.

The release knob in the cockpit should be positioned for the pilot's left hand, and the conventional colour for it is yellow. This avoids confusion with colours for other levers or knobs, such as for air-brakes, flaps, or trimmer.

Swallow airborne on a bungie launch. This crew is four on each side.

The motor glider

The main reason for installing an engine in a sailplane is to enable it to launch itself. Its performance as a sailplane may suffer to some extent, depending on the position of the engine, but this is not important in a motor glider intended for training. In general, there are two sorts of self-launching motor gliders: those looking more like long-winged, little aeroplanes, and those which are high performance sailplanes with a retractable engine—these are usually single-seaters. The first are used for training, or for a mixture of soaring and touring by private owners, with the engine being used much more than just for launching. The second variety are flown almost entirely as genuine sailplanes. The pilot launches himself, perhaps to fly to the mountains to soar among them, and then uses the engine again to return home to avoid an away landing. In some countries motor gliders are considered as sailplanes for legislation purposes, and in others as a simple aeroplane under different rules.

There is a third type of motor sailplane—sometimes known as a self-sustaining glider. The engine is so small and low powered that it is not capable of getting the sailplane off the ground, so the aircraft always has to be launched as a glider. The

A Scheibe SF-27 with retractable engine, of twenty years ago.

Returning to the airfield after a lesson in a motor glider.

Opposite left To fly above the clouds is a rare pleasure for a sailplane pilot. He is normally underneath.

Right The Falke SF-25 basic trainer. Span 15.2 m (50 ft), engine Volkswagen 45 hp.

The Ventus Turbo extends its 12hp 2-stroke engine to fly home when thermals weaken.

engine is used solely for enabling the pilot to fly home when he can find no more upcurrents. A sailplane with a glide angle of 1:40, or better, needs only 8 hp to keep it airborne in quiet air, while a self-launching motor glider needs 40–60 hp.

The weight of these tiny engines and the space they take up when retracted into the fuselage are small, and the effect on the performance of the sailplane is negligible. With such a self-sustaining engine the pilot can continue soaring beyond reach of his base, as long as there is some lift left in the air, without having to commit himself to landing at an airfield for an aerotow or to the complications of a trailer retrieve.

Motor gliders and training

A two-seat self-launching motor glider can be used to assist in the training of glider pilots in several ways. To begin with the student can be taken up and can learn to use the controls more quickly, because he can stay airborne until the lesson is finished. The feel of the controls may be a little different from those of a sailplane, but at this stage the objective is to get the student to understand what they do and to co-ordinate them. Circuit planning can also be speeded up as the aircraft does not have to land and wait to be re-launched between each circuit. The motor glider is also useful for teaching emergency and field landings, and later, navigation. The student endeavours to map read his way around a set course, with the in-structor using the engine to simulate thermals, or to cause the student to select a field and prepare for an outlanding.

The single-seater motor sailplane pilot usually does not aim to start his engine until it is obvious that he is going to have to land in a field. However, he may not appreciate that the decision-height for engine start-ing is actually higher than would be needed when choosing a landing field in a pure sailplane. If the pilot waits until he is down to 'sailplane' height, and then the engine does not start, he may find himself too low to reach a good field.

There are international compe-titions for motor gliders, based on the minimum use of the engine which is recorded on a special barograph. There are also world and national records in which the engine has to be stopped before crossing a start line, and not used prior to landing or crossing a finish line. Motor gliders may also be used to attempt *sail-plane* records, but only if it is not possible to re-start the engine once it has been stopped before crossing the start line. The pilot has to fly with the same disciplines and limitations as a sailplane pilot to obtain a record.

Before take off, the pilot of a motor glider should carry out the standard sailplane cockpit pre take-off check (see page 48), plus the following additions:

P Petrol on and enough for the flight.
P Propeller unfeathered or free. People clear.
T Throttle and mixture set.
I   Ignition on contact.

Part 2: Learning to Fly

Flying a sailplane is a world apart from sitting in a big jet, because you and your sailplane are partners with the air itself. Using only the air's energy you can soar long distances on your strong slender wings; and learning how to do it is fun. But it is also a serious business, needing concentration and hard work if you want to fly well.

Before you take to the air in a sailplane you may not know if you will enjoy it or not—but you never will know unless you try; so go to a club or school and have a flight with an instructor in a two-seater. Give yourself plenty of time to look around and ask all the questions you want.

Clothes

If you book to go on a course, use any spare time beforehand to read gliding books or magazines and, very importantly, think about what clothes to take. In cooler countries, like Britain, it is often colder than you expect out on an airfield; and it will probably be muddy underfoot. In warmer lands it can be dusty as well as hot, and there may be glare from bright light. As a learner you may spend most of each day out on the field, so be prepared, and be comfortable.

Fitness

You should be reasonably fit. In some countries a medical examination is required before you fly solo; in others, only a simple declaration of fitness. Nevertheless, even if you have a valid medical certificate in your pocket do not fly unless you feel well. Never fly with a hangover, or with a cold as it may make you temporarily deaf, or when taking medication—unless the doctor has confirmed that it will not affect your flying. Some prescribed drugs may make you drowsy and slow to react. Feeling fit is a personal matter and in your own interests, you should be honest with yourself.

Age

Age itself is no bar. Generally, there is a minimum age at which solo flying is permitted, ranging from 14–18, but at the older end of the scale there are usually no rules. It all depends on how mentally and physically active you are, and above all whether you have enough spare time. Older people often learn more slowly, remember things less well, and take longer to solo; but counter these disadvantages with greater general experience, spending a lot of time at the airfield, and talking gliding. If your job still takes up all your thinking time, it would be better to wait until you have more time to spare.

Out on the airfield

At the end of your first day's instruction you will probably feel close to despair, because there seemed so much to learn and you cannot remember half of it. Don't worry. This is normal and after a few days you will find that all those isolated bits of information begin to slot in to place.

The day probably started with a meeting of newcomers and a talk about the flying programme by your instructor—about how you will be expected to push sailplanes out on the field and stow them in the hangar at the end of the day, and how to do

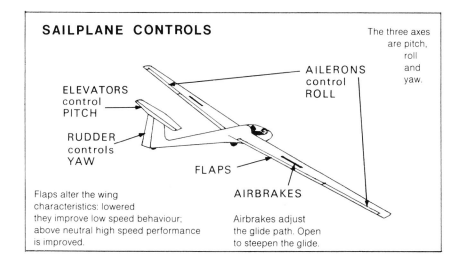

SAILPLANE CONTROLS

The three axes are pitch, roll and yaw.

AILERONS control ROLL

ELEVATORS control PITCH

RUDDER controls YAW

FLAPS

AIRBRAKES

Flaps alter the wing characteristics: lowered they improve low speed behaviour; above neutral high speed performance is improved.

Airbrakes adjust the glide path. Open to steepen the glide.

Flying clothes should be comfortable beneath harness and parachute straps.

Below In hot countries pilots susceptible to peeling noses take care.

all this without damaging anything. And you will certainly be told to keep your *eyes open* in all directions when walking on the airfield—a sailplane coming in to land cannot dodge around you at the last moment.

Next you will be shown the two-seater you will fly; you will sit in the cockpit to familiarise yourself with the position of the controls and instruments, and you will learn how to do up the shoulder harness correctly. The instructor will also show you around the outside of the sailplane to learn how the control surfaces move, how it has to be checked over to be sure that it is fit to fly and—at last—how to take it out to the launch point.

When your turn comes to fly you will climb into the cockpit (usually the front seat, with the instructor in the rear one) and do up the harness straps. Remember that these should be comfortable, but tight, to give a good feeling of security. Now rest your feet on the rudder pedals and hold the stick lightly in your right hand; your left will be used to release the launch cable, and later for operating the airbrakes or spoilers. In front of you are the instruments, and the only one that may need to be set before take off is the altimeter (to show either zero at airfield height, or height above sea level (see page 32)). Ask the instructor any questions you like.

Pre take-off checks

This is the first important action. The pre take-off, or cockpit, check must be done properly before *every* take off. Its purpose is simply to ensure

The popular Ka-13 two-seat trainer. Span 16 m (52.48 ft), glide ratio 28:1.

that when you get into the air nothing will go wrong with the aircraft. You should learn a mnemonic so that you will never forget a single item. Obviously, the most vital is C for Controls: these must all move fully and freely, and for each movement of the stick or rudder pedals there must

The new pilot flies his first few solos in the sailplane on which he learnt. Cockpit of the Ka-13.

Before allowing the cable to be attached, do the cockpit check:

C Controls—Check that elevator, ailerons, and rudder work freely, fully, and in the correct sense. If the control surfaces cannot be seen from the cockpit, a helper should be asked to check their movements.

B Ballast—See that the aircraft is correctly ballasted for the cockpit load, and check any weight restrictions.

S Straps—See that all harness straps are secure and tight.

I Instruments—Check that the altimeter is set as required (at zero or airfield height) and that other instruments are serviceable. Start barograph (if applicable).

F Flaps set for take off.

T Trim—Check operation and position of trimmer lever, for winch launch normally in middle of the range, for aero-tow further forward.

C Canopy—Check that it looks fully closed, is locked and secure, that bolts or catches are fully home, and that it does not yield to upward pressure.

B Brakes—Check that airbrakes or spoilers work freely and together, and that they are shut and locked.

Have the cable attached to the appropriate hook. And, if it is the first launch of the day, make a test release, using the words 'Open—Close—Test—Close'. Check that the take-off path is clear. Check that there is no one in front of any part of the glider, or near the tail plane. See that the wing helper is holding the wingtip corectly. Tell the signaller that you are ready to start the launch. If for any reason you do not wish to take off release the cable or rope, and shout 'stop' to the signaller.

be a corresponding and correct movement of the control surface. Once in the air there is no time to discover that a seat cushion is jamming the stick, or that someone has forgotten to connect the ailerons. See that *YOU* notice such things *BEFORE* take off.

Attaching the launch cable

After the cockpit check is complete you are ready to have the launch cable or rope attached. If it is the first launch of the day, or if the last landing was in a muddy or sandy place, the release should be checked by a helper pulling hard on the rope as you pull the release knob.

Having attached the rope you are ready to take off, provided that there are no aircraft coming in to land or on the ground ahead. Because you may not be able to see well enough all round from the cockpit you should call to the signaller by the wingtip with the words 'Clear ahead, above and behind', and when he responds 'Clear', call 'Take up slack'. The signaller now swings his bat to and fro in front of his knees and the launch driver will slowly pull the cable taut. When it is lying straight call 'All out'. The signaller will wave his bat above his head, and the launch driver will increase power to get the sailplane into the air.

For your first few flights the instructor will do the launch himself, with you following his actions with your hands and feet lightly on the controls. After releasing the cable, the instructor will adjust the attitude

of the sailplane so that it is flying at the correct airspeed—probably 40–50 knots—and so your first flying lesson begins.

The order in which you will be taught the subsequent lessons will vary according to the weather and the site, and may be different from that given here—use this book to serve as background information for each exercise.

The launch point signaller. *Take up slack.* The signaller waves the bat below his waist, while looking at the sailplane to be launched, so that he would quickly be able to stop the launch if necessary. *All out.* The signaller waves the bat above his head, still watching the sailplane. *Stop.* This signal must be as clear as possible to the now distant tow car driver.

The instructor's view of his student flying
straight at the correct attitude and airspeed.

Control of airspeed

The first lesson in the air is to learn to fly at the correct airspeed. In straight flight there is a relationship between the attitude of the sailplane (what you can see ahead over the nose of the horizon) and the reading on the airspeed indicator. You need to learn where the nose should be when you

Flying straight, and a little fast. Because sailplanes have low drag they gain speed quickly with little nose-down change of attitude.

fly faster and slower than the normal speed. You alter or adjust the airspeed by small forward or backward movements of the stick. Forward, and the nose goes down, giving a better view ahead and increasing the airspeed. When you move the stick back the nose rises, you see less ahead, and the airspeed is reduced. If you continue to fly with the nose too high the aircraft will fly more and more

slowly until it stalls. You will soon find that only small and gentle movements of the stick are needed, but do not ever concentrate on stick position; look out ahead and try to make the nose stay in the correct position in relation to the horizon. While you are practising flying at the correct attitude and airspeed the instructor will be looking after the other controls.

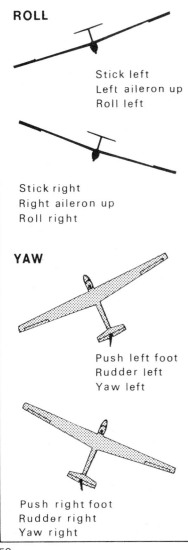

ROLL

Stick left
Left aileron up
Roll left

Stick right
Right aileron up
Roll right

YAW

Push left foot
Rudder left
Yaw left

Push right foot
Rudder right
Yaw right

Ailerons

The ailerons are controlled by sideways movements of the stick. Move it gently to the left and the left wing will go down; stick to the right lowers the right wing. If the stick is kept over to the side, bank continues to increase. To fly with the wings level the stick is central; but again, do not think about stick position. Keep looking out and around the horizon, and relate your wings to it to see when you are flying level. After all, when you drive around a corner in a car you do not think about how much you need to turn the steering wheel: you position the whole car in relation to the bend in the road.

The ailerons are the only control in which the two surfaces move differently. When you apply bank to the left, the left aileron goes up and the one on the right wing goes down. This affects the lift and the drag differently on each wing. The aileron on the inside of the turn (the upgoing surface) develops less lift but also less drag. The outer wing, on the other hand, is producing more lift and more drag. This greater drag initially tries to swing the nose against the direction of the turn. It is called *aileron drag*. Designers have reduced it by building *differential* ailerons, with the downgoing aileron not able to move down as far as the inner aileron moves up. On many sailplanes aileron drag may not be very noticeable but you should understand its cause.

Aileron and elevator together

Having tried the effects of the fore and aft and lateral movements of the stick separately, you will practise using them together—to fly at the right attitude and speed while keeping the wings level. It is the first step in the all-important co-ordination of the controls.

All too soon it will be time for the instructor to take over again to look after the landing. If you have completely lost the airfield do not worry. It is usual and you will have

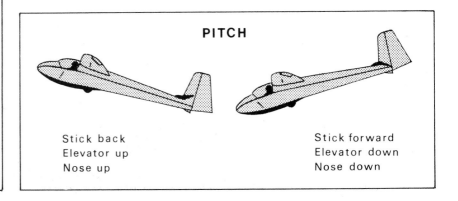

PITCH

Stick back
Elevator up
Nose up

Stick forward
Elevator down
Nose down

Pushing the two-seater back for its next launch. Sailplanes should be handled only at strong points, and never on the control surfaces.

plenty more opportunities to orientate yourself.

The rudder

If you push with your left foot, the nose of the sailplane will yaw to the left, and with your right foot it yaws to the right. But somehow the 'skiddy' feeling you get when doing this does not seem right. So what is the rudder for?

In order to turn, the wings have to be banked with the ailerons. But using ailerons alone does not produce a very efficient or tidy turn. This is because when you apply bank on its own the immediate effect is that the aircraft starts to slip sideways in the direction of the lower wing. This sideways flow over the fin and rudder then causes the nose to swing—the same principle as a weathercock—and the sailplane starts to turn in the intended direction. The disadvantage of this slip-induced turn is that it creates considerable drag and worsens the performance of the sailplane. By using ailerons and rudder together the turn is made cleanly without unnecessary drag.

Typical launch point scene. Sailplanes waiting to be launched have their into-wind wingtips weighted by tyres. Here the wind is across the runway from the left, but it is very light.

Turning

In a turn the objective is to make the nose travel smoothly around the horizon at a steady rate and at the desired airspeed. Gentle and medium turns are not difficult. Roll on as much bank as you think you will need for a medium turn—about 35°—using stick and rudder in the same direction at the same time; and check your airspeed. During the turn you will not need to keep on rudder. Come out of the turn by rolling the wings level with aileron and using some rudder to return smoothly to level flight. Check airspeed again.

Before, during, and after a turn you must look out for other aircraft.

If, during the turn, you find airspeed is increasing, keep a slight

Nose on the horizon in a gentle left turn.

A medium turn. The nose is well down to obtain a safe approach speed.

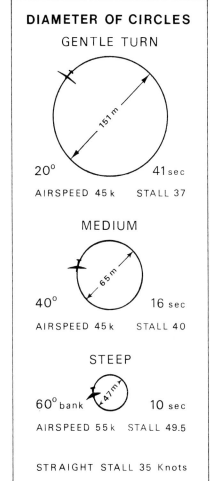

DIAMETER OF CIRCLES

GENTLE TURN

151 m

20°   41 sec

AIRSPEED 45 k   STALL 37

MEDIUM

65 m

40°   16 sec

AIRSPEED 45 k   STALL 40

STEEP

47 m

60° bank   10 sec

AIRSPEED 55 k   STALL 49.5

STRAIGHT STALL 35 Knots

back pressure on the stick to prevent this. In doing so you pull the wing to a slightly higher angle of attack to produce the extra lift needed in a turn. When you come out of the turn to fly level again, you must release any back pressure on the stick, otherwise the nose will be higher than it should be, and you may be flying too slowly.

When you have done several turns in both directions you need to become more critical about their quality. There are basically two faults in turns: (a) keeping on too much rudder during the turn, and (b) not using enough rudder as you roll into and

out of the turn. The first makes the aircraft skid outwards, like a car cornering on an icy road, and the second makes the aircraft slip inwards and downwards towards the centre of the turn. For practice, try to make as good a turn as you can, then deliberately put on too much rudder to discover what a skidding turn really feels like. Correct to a good turn, and then do a slipping turn. Producing these faults intentionally makes it easier to recognise them when they occur inadvertently.

It is very important for the sailplane pilot to be able to turn well, because continuous circling is needed to stay in thermals. If you cannot turn accurately it will be more difficult to do well unless you have given yourself plenty of practice in turning, and you understand how to correct untidy swooping turns.

Co-ordination

Some pilots take time to get it all together. You may find that you are managing to keep airspeed under control and discover that one wing is low, or you might put on the right amount of bank and be too heavy footed with the rudder. But just as you think it is all too difficult it comes right, and you feel properly in control of your flying.

Steep turns

When you are able to make reasonably accurate turns in both directions and can analyse the effect that each control has on the turn you will be ready to turn more steeply.

Increase in stall speed As soon as you turn, the stall speed begins to increase, though in gentle and medium turns this increase is sufficiently small that no extra flying speed is needed to compensate for it. The reason the stall speed rises is simply that the aircraft becomes 'heavier' and more highly loaded, because to stay in a turn it has to resist centrifugal force. As the angle of bank is steepened, and the circle diameter reduced, the load on the wings becomes greater and the stall

speed higher. In a 60° banked turn, for example, the stall speed is 1.41 times that in straight flight. If this were 35 knots it would rise to 49.5 knots in a 60° turn.

Because you will be flying steep turns at a higher airspeed than usual and, at first, you will not be achieving the accuracy you would like, be prepared to lose height. Have plenty to start with. Remember that when you are flying fast, or too fast, the controls will feel more positive, and stiffer—another reason for moving them smoothly.

In the air, roll the sailplane into a turn as normal, but with a few knots extra airspeed. Settle into flying a smooth circle. Remember that you rolled on bank with ailerons and used some rudder to help go cleanly into the turn; but that the nose tended to go down and the speed increase—this was avoided by keeping a little backward pressure on the stick. To now steepen the turn, increase bank further to 45°. The bank angle and the turn rate will increase and the nose will want to drop further. Prevent this by more backward stick. Try to keep the nose of the sailplane travelling steadily round the horizon. Do a few circles at 45° bank, and when you feel the turn is under your control, roll out to fly level. As you do so the nose will rise, unless you remembered to move the stick forwards again. Now try 45° turns in the opposite direction.

When you feel happy with 45° turns try a steeper turn at, say, 50° of bank and with just a little more spare speed. You will find that you have to use even more up-elevator to keep the nose from dropping—and the turn developing into a spiral dive.

As you make your turns steeper and the turning circle smaller, you will feel the g forces beginning to press you down into the seat.

It is not too difficult to make controlled steep turns, but it is hard to get them really smooth, both going in and coming out. If you try to turn very steeply, you may well find that the limiting factor is that the stick is as far back as it will go. This is as steep a turn as it is possible to make without diving. If, when doing steep turns, the situation seems to be getting out of hand, or you are in a muddle, *take off bank*. With the wings level, or nearly so, it will be easy to return to normal flight.

Before starting to turn, look round for other aircraft; and start with *plenty* of height—2000 ft or so. The sailplane's rate of descent increases appreciably when turning steeply, or badly.

When you can do all your turns and circles neatly and accurately you will be well on the way to becoming a soaring pilot.

The launch

Winch or car tow

For your first few flights in the two-seater the instructor will have flown the sailplane on the launch, with you keeping your hands and feet lightly on the controls. Now you will start to do the take off and launch yourself. On pages 39 and 40 the methods of winch launching and car towing were described, so refer to this if you wish to refresh your memory of what is involved.

The launch will always be made into wind, or as near to it as possible, and the strength of the wind will determine the length of the take-off run; if it is fresh you will take off almost at once. Having given the signals to launch you will find the sailplane accelerates fast, while you try to keep it running straight with rudder *and* hold the wings level with aileron. Keep the sailplane running on its mainwheel until it has enough speed to take off; do not let either the nose skid or the tail skid grate along the ground. Very quickly you will be airborne, with the sailplane trying to climb steeply. Do not let it do so until you are about 100 ft above the ground. If you do not keep control of the climb, and the cable breaks or the

Above A tow car needs a powerful engine, and should be cut down so that the observer (in the left seat) can watch the sailplane being launched. This tow car runs on propane gas.

Below The launch cable is covered with a thick plastic tube at the sailplane end to reduce the chance of catching round the wheel. The small parachute, for lowering the cable after the launch, soon wears out dragging on the ground.

Angle of the wing to the horizon on a winch launch.

launch fails for any reason, you will be left nose high in a stalling attitude. Like this, you will not have enough height to regain flying speed before striking the ground (see Cable break emergencies on page 73). So climb gently at first, and only when you are at a safe height increase the angle of climb—smoothly. During the middle part of the launch the climb angle will be quite steep, 40°–45°, and this may be checked if you can see the underside of the wing in relation to the horizon. Keep the wings level or, if there is some cross wind, keep the windward wing slightly down to prevent being drifted across the airfield.

On a winch launch, as you near the top of the launch a downward pull of the cable on the nose of the sailplane may be noticed and this should not be resisted. If you continue to hold the nose high the sailplane will start to buck up and down, which could break the cable. When no more height is being gained—or with car towing when the driver stops at the end of the runway—you lower the nose and release the cable. Give the release knob two hard pulls to be sure. After the cable has gone check your airspeed and fly on your way.

Aerotow take off with the sailplane steady and straight behind the tow plane.

58

Aerotow

Aerotowing is an excellent way of being launched for a soaring flight, as the tow pilot can leave you in a thermal or under a good-looking cloud. But it is quite difficult to do until you can control your sailplane reasonably well, because you are having to fly it *and* formate on the aeroplane.

The take-off run will be longer than on a winch launch because the tug aeroplane accelerates more slowly. As a result you need to make greater efforts to keep straight. The sailplane will take off before the tug, so as soon as you are airborne fly at a height of 7–10 ft (2–3 m) until the tug leaves the ground. Shortly after it does so it will

start to climb: and so must you. Try to keep the tow plane at all times on the horizon, with the sailplane just above the slipstream. The instructor will show you the position for the type of aeroplane being used. It is dangerous to get too high on tow as this can cause the tug to run out of elevator and dive uncontrollably. The tow pilot has some responsibility here in that he should avoid towing towards a low, dazzling sun so that you cannot see properly. He should, also, never tow into cloud. While you are being towed you will be flying at a higher airspeed than in free flight, so the controls will feel more responsive; avoid overcontrolling (see page 73, Emergencies).

During the tow the tug will need to make turns to remain near the landing field, and you must turn as well. When you see the tug start to bank into a turn, follow it round by maintaining a symmetrical back view of the aeroplane. If you start to turn too soon you will make a smaller radius turn than the tug, the tow rope will slacken and droop, and you will have to reduce bank for a few seconds to get it taut again. If you cannot do so, you will have to release. When the towplane straightens up from the turn, again do likewise, keeping the aeroplane in symmetry.

Although it is the towplane pilot's responsibility to look out for and avoid other aircraft, aeroplanes do have blind spots, so it is sensible for you to keep looking as well.

When the towplane reaches the designated height, usually 2000 ft or 700 m, you release the tow rope. But remember that if at any time the tow pilot waggles his wings, this is an order to release, and you must do so. When you release, avoid having the rope under more than usual tension, as it will spring back towards the aeroplane and flick itself into knots. This means that you must not pull up to gain a few extra feet before releasing.

After you are sure that the tow rope has gone, turn or climb away to clear. The tug pilot will watch you to make sure you are free before he dives away to return to the airfield. As soon as your airspeed is correct for normal flying go on your way, away from the airfield tow release area.

Your first few tows will be made in

AEROTOW SIGNALS

Tug rocks wings
RELEASE
AT ONCE
I have a
problem

SAILPLANE CANNOT
RELEASE. Flies out to
left and rocks wings

Tug flies
over airfield
and releases rope

Sailplane
flies in
high tow

AFTER RELEASE
Sailplane turns left

smooth air. It is much harder work to maintain position behind the tug when the air is gusty or there are many thermals: not only are both aircraft affected by the turbulence, but both are unlikely to be in air that is behaving the same way at the same time. Once, however, you have got the feel and rhythm of aerotowing—and you will—it is a highly satisfactory way to get into the air.

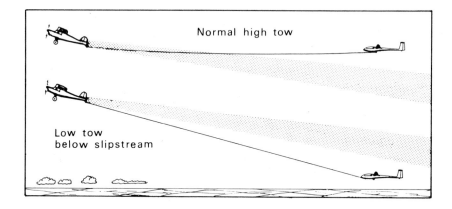

Normal high tow

Low tow
below slipstream

Getting back on the ground

Getting back on the ground again should be considered in two stages:
1 Positioning the sailplane so that it is at the right height and in the right place to make the final approach and landing into wind. (This is circuit planning and comes later on page 68.)
2 Flying the final approach and putting the sailplane neatly on to the ground. This final approach and the landing are a continuous process, and when the approach is right, it is not difficult to make a good landing.
For various reasons, including turbulence near the ground, airspeed on the approach should be higher than that for normal flying. In calm air an increase of 5 knots may be enough, but in very gusty air even an extra 20 knots may not be adequate (see page 69, Wind gradient).

The objective in landing is to put the sailplane on the ground heading into wind. This is achieved by flying straight towards the chosen landing place with enough airspeed to be able to alter the attitude of the sailplane from that of the nose low final glide to that at which it will sit on the ground on its main wheel and tail skid. If the approach airspeed is insufficient, the sailplane will drop on to the ground with its nose still somewhat down; and if the airspeed is too high at the moment of touch down, the sailplane will bounce into the air again.

To begin with, start the final straight approach with plenty of height (250–300 ft) so that you have time to settle down at your proper

approach speed and look out for other aircraft. Have a look, too, at the windsock to make sure the wind has not changed direction.

Now look well ahead, while gliding down steadily, and as the ground approaches gently and smoothly ease the stick back to flatten gradually the glide path. Finally, try to keep flying just above the ground by bringing the stick further and further back until the sailplane lands itself. Keep it running straight ahead using rudder, and keep the wings level, until you stop.

The two most common reasons for making an untidy or bumpy landing are:
1 you did not keep the wings quite level on the final approach, so the sailplane started turning and landed slightly out of wind; and
2 you were not looking far enough ahead. It is easy on your first few landings to become mesmerised by the ground rushing past close underneath, so that your eyes are drawn downwards to focus on tussocks of grass. You may also find yourself unconsciously trying to hurry the sailplane on to the ground before it is ready to land. So relax, fly at the right airspeed, look well ahead, and move the controls smoothly.

Airbrakes and spoilers

On the final approach and landing just described there was no mention of that essential aid to landing any sailplane: the airbrakes. This was because for your first few attempts the instructor will use them to allow

LANDING

the higher sailplane must keep clear

you to concentrate on the landing itself.

Almost all sailplanes are fitted with airbrakes (see page 17). When opened they increase the drag so that the nose has to be lowered to maintain the same airspeed. This steepens the glide path. Spoilers do exactly the same thing but are not as powerful or effective as airbrakes, although they are quite adequate for slow, low performance gliders.

When you first start to use the airbrakes on the approach, make sure that you have enough height and speed to give plenty of margin for experiment. Open the airbrakes about half way, hold them in this position, and notice their effect. You will have to lower the nose to maintain your speed, but you will also be able to see ahead better over the nose. Look well ahead to where you want to land. If you think you are going to be too high, open the brakes

About to land neatly, mainwheel and tailskid together. The sailplane is ready to sink gently just above the ground.

Approaching to land into wind. The pilot uses airbrakes to steepen the glide path.

more, but if you think that your glide path is now too steep and you may land short, partly close them. If you still think you may land short, close them altogether. With practice you will be able to adjust the approach path so that you can land every time with about half airbrake. Landing without any airbrake is more difficult, as the angle you approach the ground is flat and the sailplane floats along, seemingly not wanting to land. If you use full airbrake, the airspeed will decay rapidly as you round out to land, and the sailplane may drop on to the ground before you are ready for it to do so.

Until you are used to using airbrakes do not keep moving them during the final approach. The constantly changing glide path makes it more difficult to judge the landing, and if you open them just before touch down you will be dumped unceremoniously on the ground.

After landing open the air brakes fully to prevent the sailplane leaving the ground again. When stopped, close and lock them.

Airbrakes by mistake

The biggest problem you can have with airbrakes is for them to come open unexpectedly. The most likely time for this to happen is at or shortly

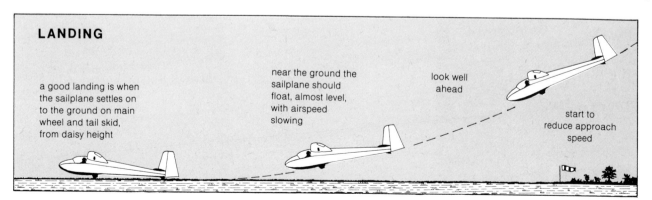

LANDING

a good landing is when the sailplane settles on to the ground on main wheel and tail skid, from daisy height

near the ground the sailplane should float, almost level, with airspeed slowing

look well ahead

start to reduce approach speed

after take off and is usually because you did not do your cockpit check thoroughly. Even if they are only unlocked and appear closed, they will suck out during the launch. If this happens you will gain little height on a winch launch, and if on aerotow the tug pilot may have to ditch you, by releasing his end of the rope so that he can retain enough flying speed to clear obstructions ahead. It is a silly way to break an expensive sailplane. If you think something is not quite right look out sideways to see if the airbrakes are open.

While waiting to take off there is plenty of time to do a thorough cockpit check.

Circuit planning

How are you going to land on this airfield? In which direction? Where is the wind blowing from? Can you see any other aircraft?

So far you have been learning to control the sailplane in the air, with the instructor taking all the planning and positioning decisions. He has looked after getting you into the right place from which to start your approach and landing, and has watched out for other aircraft. He will have told you to look out and around, but you have probably been concentrating so hard on flying at the right speed, or on turns, that you have not had time to look anywhere at all. But now that you are able to make the sailplane do what you want—at least most of the time—you are ready to take planning decisions for yourself; and the first step is to plan your circuit of the airfield so that you will arrive at the right place and height for your final approach and landing.

It is sensible that all aircraft using an airfield should follow a known circuit pattern. This is usually in the form of a 'square' left-handed circuit, with each leg used progressively to prepare the pilot for his landing. If a normal left-hand pattern is in use, and you are launched by winch or tow car, you will release over the upwind end of the airfield at around 800–1000 ft. As soon as the cable has gone:

○ Check your airspeed is correct.
○ Locate yourself in relation to the airfield.
○ Look around for any other aircraft—even balloons.

Now turn left on to the first leg, to fly cross wind, but keep upwind of the airfield boundary. If the wind is fresh you will need to point the nose to some extent into it, so that you track along the intended flight path. If this is not done you will drift back over the airfield. If you are still above 600 ft, use up some height by flying away from the circuit.

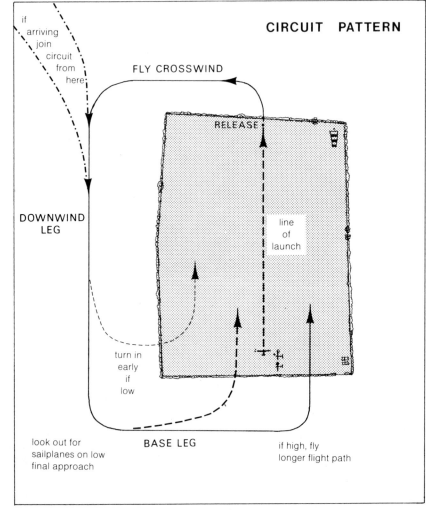

CIRCUIT PATTERN

if arriving join circuit from here

FLY CROSSWIND

RELEASE

line of launch

DOWNWIND LEG

turn in early if low

look out for sailplanes on low final approach

BASE LEG

if high, fly longer flight path

Never come in to land over the top of parked aircraft. If you undershoot you have no engine to help you clear them.

Downwind leg

Continue flying cross-wind until you are a little beyond the airfield, *but do not lose sight of it*, then turn downwind. You will now easily see all of the landing field and can plan the important stages of the circuit. In a sailplane, gliding down at a steady rate, your objective is to fly the *distance* needed to position it for the final approach. So on this downwind leg you must decide whether you are higher, or lower, than you expect or want to be. If high, turn gently on to a slightly divergent path from the airfield. If low, keep closer but do not get on top of the field so that you do not have room to make your next two turns.

While on this downwind leg have a good look at the landing area to check that it is, and is likely to remain, clear of aircraft or retrieve vehicles. Check on the windsock: are you being blown away from the field or towards it? Is the direction still the same as it was at take off, or has it

changed—or is the wind now stronger? On some days of strong convection the wind may alter in minutes. Are you flying through lift or in sink? On this downwind leg you should have enough height to make quite big alterations, and to correct the alterations if you need to. If the wind is strong your groundspeed on this downwind leg will be fast, so you may not have much *time* to carry out the downwind checks. These include:
○ Check that your harness straps are tight.
○ Stow any cameras or maps.
○ Check instruments are reading normally.
○ Lower landing wheel (if retractable—and if retracted!)
○ Look round for other aircraft.
Looking round should not only be a check on other aircraft flying in the circuit, but for sailplanes coming in low on final glide from a long way out. Never forget that a sailplane cannot gain height like an aeroplane, and its pilot may have only just enough

height to get into the landing field— from *any* direction.

Base leg

When you arrive at a point a little downwind of the field, though not too far if the wind is strong, look around and turn on to base leg. You are now again flying cross wind, and possibly drifting *away* from the airfield. If you do not think that you have height to spare, turn in a little more than 90° so that you track along parallel to the boundary. The base leg is where you make fine adjustments to achieve the right position and height for the final approach. As you are now becoming closer to the ground, it is also the point at which airspeed should be increased to that appropriate for the conditions. If the air is calm a few knots extra will be enough, but if the wind is rough and gusty an increase of 15 knots or so may be needed. This is an important judgement which has to be made, but remember that at higher airspeeds the sailplane's rate of descent will increase. While on this leg put your hand ready on the airbrake lever.

When you are nearing the into-wind line along which you intend to make the final approach, turn smoothly into wind. If, however, before you reach this point you think you are lower than you should be, turn in early and land on the near side of the intended finals line. Never allow yourself to get into a situation whereby you are still turning as the ground arrives!

After turning on to finals, check your approach speed as usual, use airbrakes as necessary, and look well ahead to prepare for landing.

Airspeed and groundspeed

If the air were always windless there would be few problems in flying, particularly near the ground; but it is not, and there are several ways the wind can confuse or frustrate your plans. Firstly, remember that airspeed is the speed of the aircraft through the air, and is not the same as the speed at which the sailplane covers the ground (groundspeed), unless there is no wind at all. The wind is a mass of air which is moving along, and if you are flying in it your aircraft will be carried along at the wind speed regardless of the direction in which it is pointing. If your airspeed is 50 knots and you are flying *with* a 15-wind your speed over the ground will be 65 knots. If you fly against this wind your airspeed will still be 50 knots but your ground-speed only 35 knots. If the wind is very strong, say, at 45 knots, your ground-speed when flying into it will be a very slow 5 knots; so you would be flying over the same fields for a long time—and might well have to land in them.

Drift

If, on a day of no wind, you fly straight towards a distant landmark you will in due course arrive at it, still flying straight in the same direction. If, however, there is a wind blowing across your route it will drift you sideways and downwind of your intended track over the ground. If you continue to point at the distant land-mark you will eventually reach it, but from an almost downwind direction because you will have to keep alter-ing your heading to keep pointing towards it. To avoid wastefully flying this extra distance you should start by heading sufficiently upwind of the landmark, so that you will track over the ground in a straight line towards

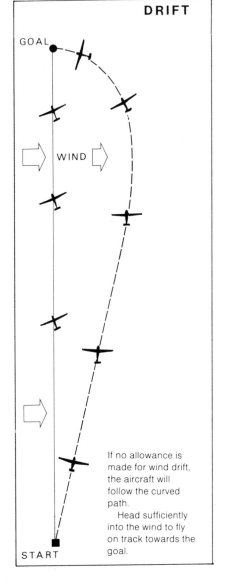

DRIFT

If no allowance is made for wind drift, the aircraft will follow the curved path.

Head sufficiently into the wind to fly on track towards the goal.

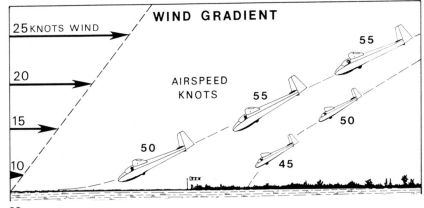

WIND GRADIENT

25 KNOTS WIND

20

AIRSPEED KNOTS

15

10

55

55

50

50

45

it. The amount needed to offset the drift in this way can be calculated (see page 92) or estimated. This is more practicable in a sailplane because during a soaring flight you will have to set off on a new heading after every thermal and use a different amount of offset each time. With practice it is possible to become very good at estimating drift and knowing how much to allow for it.

Wind gradient

At several hundred feet above the ground the wind blows at its true speed, but with decreasing height its speed lessens due to the frictional effect of the surface and the obstructions on it. This is known as *wind gradient*. On a windy day the wind may decrease in strength from, say, 20 knots at 150 ft to only 10 knots at 10ft. When the sailplane descends into this reducing wind strength relatively quickly it suffers some loss of energy, and airspeed. In fresh winds you must approach with plenty of spare airspeed so that if the wind gradient is sharp you will still be left with enough to make a proper landing. If you make the approach at slightly too slow a speed, and run into a strong wind gradient, the sailplane will lose energy to such an extent that even if you now put the nose well down you will not be able to gain any more speed.

Landing crosswind

Your first circuits and landings will have been done in easy conditions, straight into a light or steady breeze and not into a low or dazzling sun. When you have made several such circuits satisfactorily, and begin to feel in charge of the sailplane—instead of it being the boss—you will be ready to attempt landings with the wind blowing across the landing run.

If you are approaching with the wind coming from, say, the left of the intended landing run, you will find that you have to keep the nose to the left (towards the wind), otherwise you will drift away to the right. Until you get used to it the sensation is peculiar, because the sailplane is not going in the direction it is pointing. In fact, to begin with, you may even have some difficulty in deciding which way you are going. You have to decide whether or not the sailplane is flying along the intended path, and if you find that it is drifting off, you must turn more into wind.

What about the landing itself? If you carry on, with the nose off to the left of the direction the aircraft is travelling over the ground, there will be a sideways jerk as it touches down. To avoid this you have to fly the last part of the glide with the windward wing somewhat down, and just before landing you should swing the nose downwind (to the right) with rudder. This will enable the sailplane to point—and move—over the ground in the same direction. After landing keep the windward wing down to stop the wind getting under

it, and concentrate on keeping straight. The sailplane will want to weathercock into the wind during the later part of the landing run, and you must prevent it doing so.

There is no substitute for practice in cross-wind landings, and it is a skill which may often be needed when making outlandings in fields.

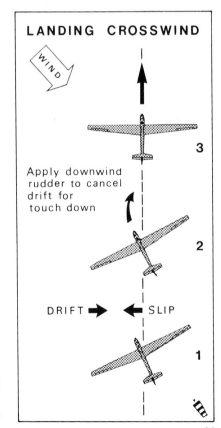

LANDING CROSSWIND

WIND

3

Apply downwind rudder to cancel drift for touch down

2

DRIFT ➡   ⬅ SLIP

1

Learning about emergencies

Suddenly a Libelle appears close. Why did you
not see it earlier?

Some people think that nothing will go wrong for them in the air, but it occasionally does. Without warning you may have to cope with a cable break on the launch, a near collision, or an obstructed landing place. What would you do if the aircraft going in to land ahead of you broke its landing gear, and became immobile just where you wanted to go? During your flying training you will be taught how to cope with these sorts of problems, but the best insurance against being caught out by the unexpected is to think about what could go wrong, and try to imagine what you would do about it.

Stalling inadvertently

Maybe you are sure that you would never let a sailplane stall by mistake—then one day it does. Fortunately, there is plenty of height, but how could it have happened? Was it because you were too confident, or were concentrating on something else—or had not learnt well enough how a sailplane behaves when flying near the stall?

Before you solo the instructor will give you several opportunities to fly at a safe height as slowly as you possibly can so that you will recognise how the sailplane behaves shortly before it stalls. On page 51

the symptoms were described: a sloppy feel to the controls, the nose high so you cannot see so well ahead, different or less airflow noise over the canopy. On some aircraft there may also be a noticeable buffeting on the tail as it is hit by the increasingly turbulent air from the wing. Do not forget, as well, the increased rate of descent.

When you have practised recognising these symptoms, the next step is to fly slower still, stall deliberately and learn how to recover with the minimum loss of height. If you stall when flying straight, the nose will drop—gently if you approach the stall gently, and sharply if you pull the stick back to raise the nose high. In each case the ensuing dive will give you back the speed the sailplane needs to fly, but more height will be lost from a sharp stall than from a gentle one. Sailplane types vary in their stall behaviour and the amount of height they will lose, but 100 ft before being able to return to normal attitude and speed should be taken as a minimum—and a good reason for flying with enough airspeed when near the ground.

If you are turning, or if rudder is applied, when you are flying close to the stall the wing on the inside of the turn will stall first, because it is flying at a greater angle of attack. When the inner wing stalls it will drop, and the outer wing, still flying, will help rotate the sailplane. If this process is allowed to continue the sailplane will spin.

In training you will practice in the two-seater to learn how they can

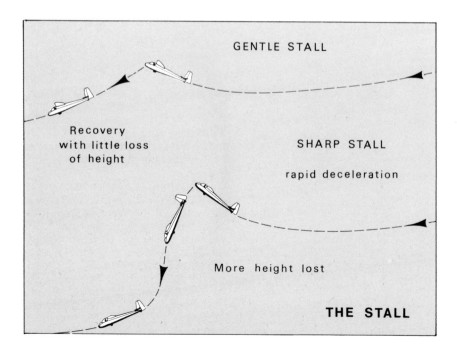

GENTLE STALL

Recovery with little loss of height

SHARP STALL

rapid deceleration

More height lost

THE STALL

occur, what they feel like, and how to recover without losing any more height than is necessary. But later, when you are solo, you will want to practise recovering to normal flight before the incipient spin develops into a full spin. This you do by immediately getting the nose down to gain speed, and picking up the drooping wing with opposite rudder. If you try to stop it dropping with aileron alone, this will simply add to the drag on the inner wing and to the lift of the outer wing, and will encourage the spin. You may notice that the inner wing starts to feel heavier just before the sailplane

stalls. This is a warning sign to remember.

Should the sailplane spin fully—or you wish to spin it—the rotation will develop with the nose well down, with each full turn of the spin taking only a few seconds. This feels very fast, and if you have spun by mistake it can be disorientating, so you may lose a few seconds dithering before taking the proper recovery action. Height lost in each full turn is about 300 ft.

The manner in which an aircraft spins varies with different types. Some spin steadily with the nose well down, others oscillate in pitch. Usually, the ASI shows quite a low speed

which remains constant during the spin. Recovering from a spin demands knowing and applying a well learnt drill—even though some aircraft may recover as soon as you make any control movement at all. Others do not come out so easily, so the reason for the drill is to ensure that you do what is necessary in the correct sequence; otherwise one of the tail surfaces may be in the dead air of the other one. In a spin the aircraft is not moving in the direction of its nose but yawing about, which means the airflow is not moving over the aircraft in a normal manner.

The recovery drill is:
○ Full opposite rudder (ailerons central).
○ Stick steadily forwards *until* the spinning stops.
○ Centralise controls and pull out of the dive.

This should be done without delay, but *smoothly*. A sailplane is very clean and accelerates rapidly. It is easy to fly too fast and overload the wings by pulling sharply out of a high speed dive. The airbrakes should be opened before the speed gets too high.

Quite often, what started off as a spin changes into a spiral dive after a turn or so. The sensation is not dissimilar as the aircraft is rotating in an unusual way, but there are important differences. Firstly, the airspeed begins to increase rapidly, the load on the controls increases, and you may feel pressed into your seat by 'g'. If this happens the airbrakes must be opened immediately otherwise the speed will become excessive. Take

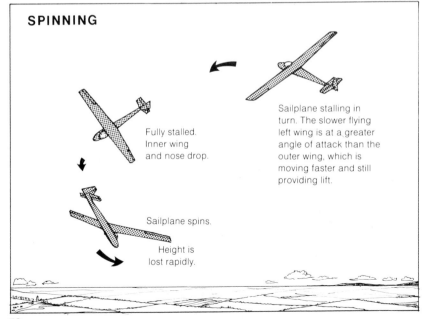

SPINNING

Sailplane stalling in turn. The slower flying left wing is at a greater angle of attack than the outer wing, which is moving faster and still providing lift.

Fully stalled. Inner wing and nose drop.

Sailplane spins.

Height is lost rapidly.

off bank, and pull out gently.

It is useful to have tried opening the airbrakes at high speed before doing spins or aerobatics. On some sailplanes a substantial pull force may be needed to open the brakes, which must then be changed to a push force to prevent them coming fully open with a violent jerk.

Cable breaks

On every launch the pilot should be prepared for the winch or tow car cable to break suddenly, or for the engine to lose power. If the cable snaps you must get the nose down at once to gain plenty of speed: enough for an approach to land, because this is what you are about to do. Pull the release knob *hard* a couple of times to be sure of getting rid of your end of the broken cable. Now think!

If the cable has broken shortly after take off you will have no thinking time and no choice but to land straight ahead, or within a few degrees of either side of straight ahead to avoid an obstruction or rough ground. If you are higher when the sailplane is suddenly left nose high without any power, it is more difficult to decide correctly what to do—after having got the nose down, gained speed, and released the cable end. You have two choices: to turn back and make a quick low circuit to land somewhere in the middle of the field, or to find a clear space or field somewhere ahead into wind, and land there. The height at which it is safe to make a circuit is obviously greater than that needed to find somewhere ahead; the risk in at-

tempting a circuit is that you may not have enough height to get all the way round and are still turning as you land. Your instructor will tell you what is the minimum circuit height, as this will depend both on the size of the landing field and the performance of the sailplane you are flying. In a year or so, when you may have a sailplane with a glide angle of 50:1, you could turn back and fly a safe circuit from a lower height than is possible in a school two-seater.

If you are below the safe height for a circuit, you must look for a large clear space ahead, on or off the airfield, and then turn immediately away to one side of the launch line. This gives you a longer flight path to use up any excess height you may have, and a chance to study how best to make an approach. Look once more at where you intend to land, and turn back again towards the launch line so that you are on the equivalent of the base leg of an ordinary circuit. Make sure that you are flying at your approach speed and, when you think you are about in the right position and at the right height, turn into wind towards your chosen landing place. Use airbrakes at any time you need them.

Try to fly at the proper approach speed, and not too fast. There is a real temptation in such an emergency to want to hurry back on to the ground. As you get lower make any *small* adjustments of direction needed to avoid bushes, etc., and make as good a landing as you can.

The best preparation for dealing with cable breaks is to think before

every take off, 'What will I do if the cable breaks?' Whenever you are flying study nearby fields that you might have to go for if the launch fails.

Sometimes the cable does not snap, but the winch or tow car slowly loses power. You find that you are not able to climb properly and the airspeed is declining. If this happens, release the cable quickly while you are still in a position to land on the airfield. Get the nose well down, and land ahead. If you hang on in hope, the chances are that you will arrive at the far end of the field with only about 300 ft of height, not much speed, and nowhere to go.

Negative g

On the ground the human is subjected to 1g (the force of gravity), which is why you can keep your feet on it. In the air you can increase the force of gravity on yourself, and do it quite easily. If you pull sharply out of a dive, you will be pressed into the seat, and you might even temporarily black out as the blood is dragged down from your head. Pulling out of a dive in this way also puts a heavy load on the sailplane, and in an extreme case could pull the wings off.

It is also possible to subject yourself to the opposite force, negative g, and to become weightless for a few seconds—as astronauts often do for several weeks. This can happen if you suddenly push the stick forward, causing you to rise up in the straps, and perhaps feel disorientated. The most likely way for it to happen is if you have an unexpected cable break, and put the stick rapidly forward to be sure of gaining speed. Some beginner pilots have done this, and confused the negative g sensation with that of being stalled—even though they were not. They then pushed the stick even harder forward, which added to the sensation but brought them perilously close to the ground. If they had recognised the feeling of negative g they would have known that they were not stalled and could have landed normally. Most instructors give student pilots a demonstration of negative g so that if they push the stick forward sharply they will realise what is happening.

Aerotow emergencies

The most likely problem is that the tow plane is unable to climb or continue the tow before either aircraft has reached a safe height. This can occur because the tug engine fails, or because you have left your airbrakes unlocked and they have opened and are creating more drag than the tug engine can cope with. Should the tug pilot decide that his situation is rapidly becoming unsafe he will first 'fan' his rudder to tell you your brakes are open. If you do not close them immediately he will rock his wings. This is an *order* for the sailplane pilot to release. There may not be much ahead to land on but the sailplane, with its flatter glide, slower stall speed and good pilot view, is in a better position to deal with this emergency than the tow pilot; so release at once. Should the tow rope break, or the tug pilot does not even have time to rock

his wings but is obviously in difficulties, you must release at once and do the best with what height you have. Unless the tow has become very slow you should have a little extra speed that you can turn into height.

There is another emergency that can be created by the sailplane pilot. If you get out of position too high behind the tow plane, you can cause it to run out of elevator control. If this happens the tow plane will be put into a steep dive from which the pilot cannot recover. If you are high on tow, and the tug pilot releases his end of the rope, do not be surprised; and do not forget to release it at your end as well. If *you* get high, or lose sight of

the tug, or the rope goes very slack you must release *immediately*. If you understand this hazard it is easier to make considerable efforts to avoid it.

Cockpit weights and loads

Although not an emergency in itself, the pilot can create one for himself if he flies his sailplane with its centre of gravity outside the limits, or if the cockpit load is too great. Every sailplane should have a notice in the cockpit stating both the maximum and minimum cockpit loads. If these are obeyed then the c.g. will be within limits, and the aircraft will handle properly in the air.

If the c.g. is too far forwards (the

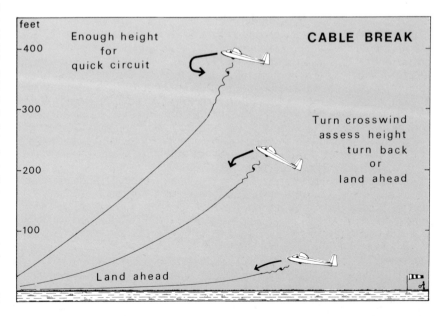

feet

CABLE BREAK

Enough height for quick circuit
—400

—300

Turn crosswind assess height turn back or land ahead

—200

—100

Land ahead

cockpit load is too heavy) the sail-plane will glide well, but in weak conditions will sink back to earth more rapidly than when flown by a light pilot. More importantly, the very

heavy pilot may run out of elevator control and have some difficulty in rounding out smoothly when landing.

The very light pilot has greater problems: if he is flying very close to the aft limit the sailplane may feel

slightly unstable and less pleasant to fly. If it is flown with the c.g. too far aft it will stall more readily, and if it is spun the recovery will be slower; in an extreme case it may not recover at all. Lightweight pilots *must* carry ballast to bring the cockpit load up to at

Do not give yourself an unnecessary emergency by coming in to land too low and too slow. At best it will result in a heavy landing.

least a little more than the minimum required. The instructor will advise on how to make up a personal ballast pack, usually with lead sheet or shot. You should not fly without it (see page 19).

Look out—once again

Some people whose eyesight is only average seem to notice everything, while some eagle-eyed pilots notice nothing. This is usually because they have not trained their eyes and brain to observe and process what moves across their vision. When you are flying and looking at the sky your eyes tend not to focus very much on anything, so you will easily miss a small aeroplane or glider a few miles away, even though it is coming in your direction. To see, and *notice*, distant aircraft you have not only to scan the whole sky regularly, but pause in your head movements at frequent intervals during the scan to focus on each bit of sky. It takes practice to focus your eyes deliberately, but it is useful to become good at it.

Peripheral vision is what you see 'out of the corner of your eye'. You use it unknowingly in the judgement of when to round out on landing, but it does not necessarily inform you about the significance of distant specks in the sky. Do not only keep turning your head, but move your eyes in your head as well. If you wear glasses, check how much the rims interfere with what you can see; and always carry a spare pair when flying. Dark sun glasses are valuable against glare, but too many pilots continue to wear them even when the light has become poor. Do not create unnecessary emergencies for yourself.

First solo

One day, after the instructor has had one or two flights with you, and you are beginning to feel that it is all coming together, he will send you on your first solo flight. He will get out, do up the straps in his cockpit so that they cannot get in the way of the controls, put in any necessary ballast, and probably say little more than 'OK, go and do a circuit like the one you just did'. He may add that without his weight the sailplane will climb a little faster and descend at a slightly slower rate. He should not have to say anything about the wind or the weather, because if there are any doubts about this he will not send you off on your own for the first time.

To you, at this moment, flying without the comforting presence of the instructor may seem a great big event and you will probably feel apprehensive; but all too soon you will be airborne and concentrating, as usual, on making yet another ordinary circuit—and all too soon you will be back on the ground. However, you are now a pilot in your own right; and you can start learning to be a better one. Statistically, the first few solo flights are some of the best a pilot makes. Later, as confidence grows, it seems to become easier to make mistakes.

Depending on the laws of the country you may be required to hold a glider pilot licence, or have your skill measured by national or international proficiency standards, Whichever it is, you will need to do some ground study to supplement your flying skills. Subjects include

First solo coming in to land, airbrakes open.

principles of flight, meteorology, basic navigation, and air law. For most people this last is the least interesting, but it is essential, because as a pilot you will share the air with other pilots. You rely on them to know the rules of the air—and they rely on you. Most clubs and schools

The K-8 is a safe and easy sailplane for the early solo pilot to fly and build up air time.

have a study programme prepared, so you will probably have been started on this some time before your first solo.

Now that you have begun to fly on your own, your objective is to consolidate and improve your flying skills. In addition to having check flights with your instructor, the best way to do this is to fly as often and regularly as

you can; and to give yourself a definite exercise to practise on each flight. After landing, go over in your mind what you did, and be honest about how well—or how badly—you fared. Flying regularly at this stage means at least every weekend for a few months, so that your flying has a good chance of becoming both instinctive and accurate.

It may have been fun learning to fly, but soaring is even more enjoyable. There is great satisfaction to be had from finding, and using, the air's free energy to fly several hundred kilo-

Soaring among mountains is beautiful, but the pilot needs to understand how the air behaves around the peaks.

metres, and hours later to return home from the sky.

The ocean of air in which you fly is, like the sea, never still. Within it there is every kind of movement, from the huge air masses of depressions and anticyclones to tiny local currents. It is the latter which interest sailplane

pilots, particularly the various ways in which air rises. Over the years pilots have discovered most of them.

A sailplane will soar when it flies in air which is rising as fast, or faster, than it is sinking to earth. If the minimum sink rate of a sailplane is 1.6 knots, the air it is flying in needs to

Fresh winds are good for hill and wave soaring. The low level wind is strongest just above the crest of the ridge.

way for the new pilot to build up plenty of air time quite quickly.

Large, fast, competition sailplanes are less suited to ridge soaring, particularly over small hills. This is because their radius of turn is too large to enable them to stay in the lift for more than part of each turn. Nevertheless, some top pilots enjoy the challenge. In parts of the world where there are great mountain

rise at this rate for the sailplane to maintain its height. Fortunately, most upcurrents are more powerful; under a growing thunderhead the air will be rising at 10 knots or more.

Hill soaring

Although most soaring is now done on thermals, these warm rising currents of summer were not understood in the early days of gliding. Instead, pilots stayed aloft in the wind as it rose up over hills, known as hill, ridge, or slope soaring. It was satisfying to the pioneers, as it allowed them to remain airborne for as long as the wind blew on to the hill. Naturally, it encouraged endurance records, but after a few years these were discontinued when pilots fell asleep in the air on flights of over *two* days. The limitation of slope soaring is that flying is tied to the narrow band of lift over the hill. Today, slope soaring may be used during training to extend the length of the flight, if the landing field is close to a suitable ridge—often the case with gliding clubs which began life in the old hill-soaring days. It is also an excellent

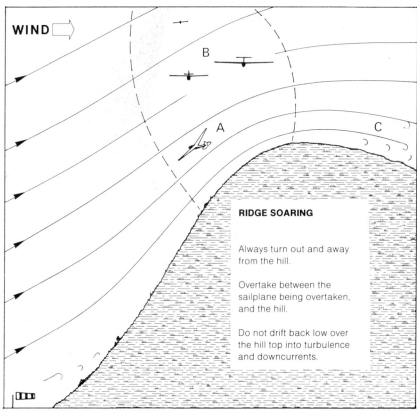

WIND

B

A

C

RIDGE SOARING

Always turn out and away from the hill.

Overtake between the sailplane being overtaken, and the hill.

Do not drift back low over the hill top into turbulence and downcurrents.

Lenticular clouds in wave produced by the Pennine hills.

ranges, such as the Appalachians in the USA, pilots have developed high speed ridge soaring so well that several world distance records have been broken in recent years.

Since many sailplanes, and sometimes hang gliders as well, may be soaring close together over the same ridge, there are some essential rules for the avoidance of collision. The first is that pilots should always turn outwards from the hill, into wind. This is a commonsense rule because turning downwind would not only be to turn towards the hill, but to risk flying into the downcurrents behind it. The second rule follows on from the first: a pilot must overtake between the hill and the glider being overtaken so that its pilot is free to turn whenever he needs to.

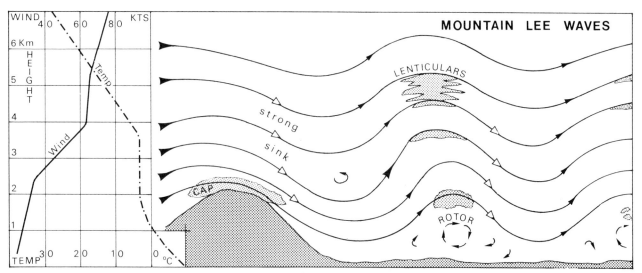

Wave soaring

As the air flows over a mountain, or range of mountains, it sometimes sets up a huge atmospheric wave system, similar to the comparatively minute undulations which occur downstream of a rock in a fast flowing river. If conditions are right (see page 81), the wave system will become well established. Waves are used by sailplane pilots to climb to heights as great as 46,000 ft (the world record). If the wind strength and direction become marginal or change, the wave system may alter or break down.

Although wave systems may develop in clear air, and without visible cloud may be difficult to locate, they are usually apparent because of the characteristic lenticular clouds they produce. These are smooth-edged, and lie in bars across the wind. They are further typified through remaining substantially over the same place on the ground, being 'anchored' to the mountain which is creating them.

Sometimes it is possible to see cloud particles flowing through the lenticular as the cloud forms continually on the windward side, and dissolves to leeward. If the air is very moist, lenticular clouds may spread to cover much of the sky, with only narrow bars of blue to show the region of the downgoing air in each wave.

Wave systems also produce other typical clouds. A cap cloud may develop over the crest of the mountain which is creating the system, and this also stays put. To the lee of the mountain, and quite low down, ragged turbulent clouds or cloudlets may be seen. These are formed in the rotating air—the rotor—where the bottom of the wave is close to the ground and its obstructions. The air in the rotor may be so wild that it is not possible to keep control of the aircraft.

Some wave systems, whose habits and reliability are known, are popularly used to make high flights for records and international badges. Often the best waves occur in the winter, which is fine for those who want to fly all the year round. In Scotland wave lift up to 20,000 ft or more occurs fairly often, and in New Zealand, Switzerland, and the USA there is excellent wave flying.

Wave lift is characteristically smooth, with rates of climb of 500 ft/min or more, so it may not take long to reach 15,000 ft – 20,000 ft; but it takes much longer to get down again. This must be taken into account when finding good wave in the late afternoon, as the sun sets on the ground some 25 minutes before it does at a height of 20,000 ft. You may be flying in glorious sunshine without a care in the world until you notice lights beginning to sparkle on the ground far below. Another problem is that it is not uncommon late in the day for low cloud to develop a few hundred feet above the surface. If you do not notice this in time, you will have to find your way down through it—without knowing how close to the ground it is. Even with radio to find out may not prevent you blundering into high ground.

Thermal soaring

Thermals are the warm air upcurrents that rise in great profusion on a good summer day; their presence is often made visible by cumulus clouds which develop in them. Thermals provide most of the world's opportunities for cross-country soaring. In temperate climates, like Britain, they are usable—though not always good—from March to October. In lower latitude countries, such as

82

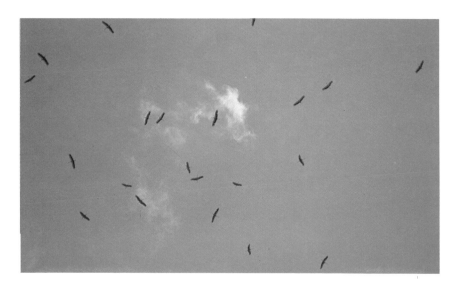

Storks circling in a thermal, with the new cumulus forming above them

The sailplane pilot uses thermals by circling up within the rising bubble, which may be anything from 100m to 1 km or more across. When he reaches the top, or the strength of the upcurrent weakens and dies, he flies off to look for another one. Thermal soaring is a mix of pilot techniques and meteorological knowledge and will be covered in much more detail on pages 103 and 104.

Heading for a cumulus growing above the mountain peaks at 10,000 ft.

Australia and Brazil, thermals are stronger and cloud base is higher. Thermals develop as a result of the heating of the earth's surface, which in turn warms the air in contact with it. When the blob or bubble of air is large and warm enough it will start to rise, and in doing so will become less dense, expand, and cool. When the temperature of the air in the thermal becomes equal to that of the surrounding air it will not rise any further. Thermal distribution follows no regular pattern because different sorts of surface (towns, marshes, forests) warm up at different rates. After breaking away from the surface thermals drift with the wind; and since their initial rate of climb is low, they may travel several miles from their source before being found and used by the pilot.

Local soaring

When you were flying dual the instructor may sometimes have used thermals, and gained height, to prolong the training flight. Somehow he seemed to know exactly where they could be found and how to centre quickly in the lift. On your own the sky seems a big place with random cumulus above and random fields below, with invisible and elusive thermals occupying the space in between. So how can you find a thermal before you are again down to circuit height and have to land? Fortunately, there is a good chance on a summer day that a thermal will find you. If you do not then let it slip through your fingers, so to speak, it will give you enough extra height—and time—to explore around and find some thermals for yourself.

The first time you fly into a thermal you will probably feel the sailplane surge and lift as it flies into the rising air. The airspeed slightly increases as a result of the energy input, and the audio variometer note rises. Then everything goes quiet again as you fly out of the far side of the lift. Next time you must react more quickly, and turn in the right direction.

Since most thermals are roughly circular in shape you stay in them by circling, if possible, in the strong centre, or core. But which way is it—to the left, to the right, or straight ahead? The first clue comes from the surge as you enter the lift. This surge is energy provided by the upcurrent, and if it is ahead it will push up the nose. If to one side it will push up that wing. So push the wing down again and turn towards it. The diagrams

show some ways of getting into thermals, but with experience you will develop techniques for yourself.

It is important to try to fly accurately. Keep your airspeed as constant as possible, particularly when circling, because for a given angle of bank your airspeed determines the size of circle you will make. If it is steady you will be making circles of the same size, so if the lift is still to one side it will be easier to shift your circles in the right direction. If your speed is varying all the time it will be only luck that puts you in the best lift. It often happens to begin with that you find yourself half in and half out of a thermal, with beautiful surges of lift alternating with quiet, depressing sink. When this occurs there is considerable temptation to shift your direction too quickly. If you think the thermal is more to the left, do a further identical circle to see if you get the same result. Now move the circle a little to the left, by straightening up for a few seconds just before the point you expect the lift to increase, and then by circling again. The thermal is less likely to go away than you are to lose it by impatience. It also helps to note some landmark ahead when you hit the strongest part of the lift. Next, do a few circles in your new position and assess the situation. When, or if, you are circling right in the core of a strong thermal you will know it at once—and it is exhilarating. But still go on flying as accurately as you can.

As you near the top of a thermal the lift will start to become ragged or weak, or you will have to break off

circling because you suddenly find wisps of grey cloud beginning to hang down around you! In either case you must take stock of your position in relation to the airfield, because you are not yet ready to land the sailplane safely in some strange field.

For local soaring you must make every effort to work *upwind* of the airfield, and to fly further upwind to look for thermals, particularly the first one. If you do not find it you are in a good position to enter the airfield circuit and land back; and if you do find it you are in a good position to explore the lift. If this is strong, so that you climb quickly, you will still be in reach of the field though maybe slightly downwind of it; but if the thermal is weak you will drift a long way without gaining much height. If this is happening you must leave the thermal while you are still within easy reach of the landing field. If you are downwind of the field you will have no choice but to fly straight into wind, with no opportunity to look for more lift.

If, however, your good thermal has left you above the upwind boundary of the airfield, you can again explore *into* wind because you are 'safe' in terms of landing back. Try to work upwind all the time; even five miles upwind at any height above 2000 ft will enable you to return home without any trouble.

Obviously, local soaring, and staying within reach of the field, is much easier in strong thermals than when they are weak. The latter bring the problem of knowing how far you can pursue feeble lift in the hope that it might improve (it rarely does). Another temptation is to go and join a circling sailplane some distance away, leaving your own not very good thermal to do so. Too often, its pilot is no better off than you are—and you will still have to locate the lift he is struggling to use. Before rushing off, wait until there is clear evidence that his thermal really is much better than yours, and that it will not have died by the time you get there.

If you do join other sailplanes in a thermal, it is the rule that you circle in the same direction as those who got there before you. This applies even if there is considerable discrepancy in height between you.

Give yourself as much practice as you can in soaring within reach of the airfield, and on each flight give yourself an objective: to work upwind to a certain landmark, or to stay airborne in average conditions for one hour. You may not achieve what you set out to do, but you will be better able to assess why you did not than if you had just wandered about vaguely, using any passing lift until you had to land.

Another thing to teach yourself when soaring locally is accurate control of speed, and not only when circling. The objective is to obtain the best performance from the sailplane. If you fly either slower or faster than the optimum airspeed you will worsen its glide performance, and in

weak lift this could return you to earth faster than you would like. On big cross-country flights it is essential to fly at the correct speed for every phase of the flight, so while soaring locally it is worth finding out the effect on the sailplane's performance of flying at different airspeeds.

The 'normal' speed at which you were taught to fly was that which would give you the best compromise between best glide angle and low sink rate, probably plus a few knots for safety if the air was turbulent. If you fly slightly slower than the optimum speed the sink rate improves a little, but the glide angle worsens. Slow down more and the sink rate starts to worsen as well as the glide angle. If you fly a little faster than optimum, the glide angle improves and the sink rate worsens. All the time you are soaring you should be considering whether or not you are flying at the best speed. In a thermal the slower speed (minimum sink speed) will allow you to make smaller circles nearer the stronger core of the thermal, while in between thermals you should fly a little faster. You will reach the next thermal more quickly, as well as spending less time flying through any sink you encounter. If you fly too fast the glide angle will worsen to an unproductive extent.

If, on your first few soaring flights, the conditions are so easy that you could stay up all day, do not be tempted to do so. The concentration needed to fly accurately is considerable, and because you are doing well you may not notice how tired—or cold—you are becoming. It is easy to

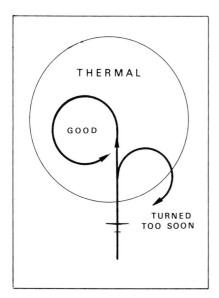

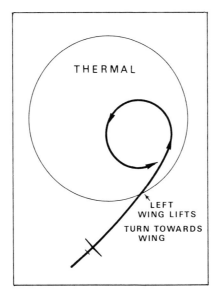

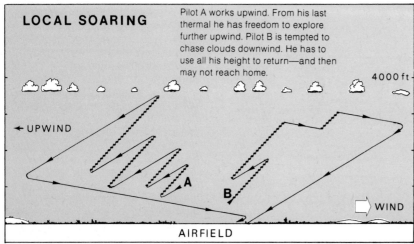

LOCAL SOARING

Pilot A works upwind. From his last thermal he has freedom to explore further upwind. Pilot B is tempted to chase clouds downwind. He has to use all his height to return—and then may not reach home.

4000 ft

← UPWIND

A

B

WIND

AIRFIELD

When joining another sailplane in a thermal, you must circle in the same direction as earlier arrivals.

forget that you have to get yourself back on the ground—in the right place and at the right speed. Do several flights of not more than one hour before becoming more ambitious. And do not forget that the easier it is for you to stay up means that a larger number of pilots will also be floating around. Keep your eyes open for them.

With several thousand feet of height you can explore for thermals away from home, but watch you do not get lost. Which way is the airfield?

When flying cross-country the sail-plane is soon out of sight of the familiar home scene, and its pilot will need to navigate with some accuracy. The world, unfortunately, is

Before take off plan what you intend to do, check maps and calculations.

too full of controlled airspace to have sailplanes, or any other aircraft, wandering about lost.

To find your way in a sailplane you need to read a map well in the air. This requires both a sense of orientation and observational skill in relating what is seen on the ground to what is presented on the paper. Soaring within reach of your landing ground should have given you plenty of opportunity to orientate yourself, to learn what the surrounding country looks like, and to identify towns

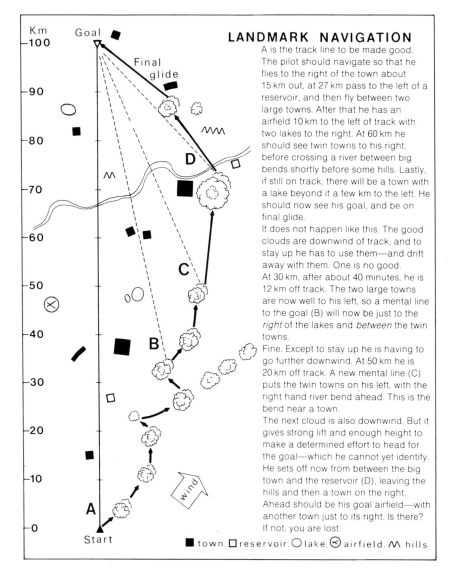

LANDMARK NAVIGATION

A is the track line to be made good. The pilot should navigate so that he flies to the right of the town about 15 km out, at 27 km pass to the left of a reservoir, and then fly between two large towns. After that he has an airfield 10 km to the left of track with two lakes to the right. At 60 km he should see twin towns to his right, before crossing a river between big bends shortly before some hills. Lastly, if still on track, there will be a town with a lake beyond it a few km to the left. He should now see his goal, and be on final glide.

It does not happen like this. The good clouds are downwind of track, and to stay up he has to use them—and drift away with them. One is no good. At 30 km, after about 40 minutes, he is 12 km off track. The two large towns are now well to his left, so a mental line to the goal (B) will now be just to the *right* of the lakes and *between* the twin towns.

Fine. Except to stay up he is having to go further downwind. At 50 km he is 20 km off track. A new mental line (C) puts the twin towns on his left, with the right hand river bend ahead. This is the bend near a town.

The next cloud is also downwind. But it gives strong lift and enough height to make a determined effort to head for the goal—which he cannot yet identify. He sets off now from between the big town and the reservoir (D), leaving the hills and then a town on the right. Ahead should be his goal airfield—with another town just to its right. Is there? If not, you are lost.

■ town. □ reservoir. ○ lake. ⊗ airfield. ᰍ hills

North is in relation to the airfield, or to become good at interpreting information presented on the map. Anytime, anywhere will do. (Which way does my house face? From which direction is the wind blowing? Why did I miss that minor road turning?)

Maps and map reading

Aviation maps, or aeronautical charts, come in two scales that are useful to the sailplane pilot. The $\frac{1}{4}$ million (approximately 4 miles/inch) for local flying and short cross-country flights, and $\frac{1}{2}$ million (8 miles/inch) for longer distances. Occasionally, the even smaller scale, 1 million (16 miles/inch), may be useful, but in populated countries may not contain enough significant detail. These scales of $\frac{1}{4}$ million, etc., may not seem to make sense in terms of inches or miles, but in metric units they are more easily understood: $\frac{1}{4}$ million is 1 cm = 2.5 km; $\frac{1}{2}$ million is 1 cm = 5 km; and 1 million is 1 cm = 10 km.

The basis of map reading navigation is to draw a line on the map from your start point to your destination (the track line); and the operating principle is that you note enough prominent landmarks on or near your track line so that you need never lose sight of one before you have identified the next one ahead. The first landmark on your route should, of course, be one that you can see before setting off. Such basic map reading requires that the visibility is reasonable, at least 10 miles (16 km), and so it should be until you have experience of five or more cross-country flights. You need to be able

and other landmarks. You should have discovered how towns can apparently disappear when covered by a dark cumulus shadow, and how motorways and rivers in valleys become hidden by rising ground when you are low.

Fortunately, it is not necessary to wait until you are airborne in an expensive sailplane to find out where

If visibility is poor you may have to check position by whatever you can see; here, the hazy sun glinting on a river ...

So just before you go, check again prominent landmarks.

to see enough landmarks to be able to relate them to each other, and to estimate the angle to your track line of motorways or railroads. There is no sense·in getting lost at this stage just because you cannot see where you are going.

Most pilots find it easier to orientate the map so that the track line points to the nose.

If you were flying cross-country in an aeroplane, you could set off from above the centre of the airfield, allow for any drift, and fly in a straight line to your destination. In a sailplane you cannot do this; not only must you search for lift, often away from your track line, and circle in it endlessly (it may seem), but you may not even be able to depart from where you took off. You may have spent an hour searching around for lift and could be several miles from the airfield. So, when you are high enough to go,

90

look for that key landmark, relate it to the airfield and to where you now are, and set off accordingly. If you can also see your next landmark in the distance, you can relate this to the first landmark and to yourself to obtain an even better idea of where you are, and which way you want to go. Although on any soaring flight you may have to fly miles to find thermals, you will not want to waste precious height flying even a short distance off course because of poor navigation.

Quite soon you will probably be looking for more lift which, when you find it, will mean more circling and concentration. Take every opportunity to note the next landmark and any other new feature you can identify, and estimate your progress in relation to them. Are you getting nearer, or drifting away, or what? Do not lose sight of key landmarks.

It is easy to become navigationally disorientated, particularly if you suddenly cannot find your best landmark because it is now in cloud shadow. Such problems can be overcome by keeping orientated in terms of the sun. In England, in summer time, the sun is almost due south at 1300 hrs, and moves roughly 15 degrees per hour. It can be used more quickly than the compass or map for giving a general sense of direction. You can straighten up from circling in your thermal with the sun, say, ahead of you on the left, knowing that you will be pointing more or less in the right direction. It will then take less time to get some precision into your navigation.

If thermals are only developing away to one side of your track line, you will soon have to work on a new one to your destination; and if it is important that you arrive there, you will have to do your best to follow it as the flight progresses. Since you are

In large, 'empty' countries a single road may be your only reliable feature.

This town (Salisbury) has a cathedral 404 ft high, which makes a good landmark.

When you are low navigation is more difficult, and good landmarks seem to disappear.

unlikely to be able to draw this modified track line on your map, you will have to visualise it in terms of landmarks. As you continue on your way look ahead and choose further landmarks, which might even be better than the ones you noted from the map. Check them on the map, as well as their relationship to other features, so you have positive identification. Continue this process as more landmarks come into view. If you are being drifted well off your original track line, make a note of features that are well downwind. When trying to stay in a thermal it is easy to forget about navigation, and then look out to find a completely strange landscape. Try to avoid this happening, because if you have to make great efforts to find yourself again it will be at the expense of locating thermals. It is a quick way to the ground.

Some pilots are reluctant to depart from their predetermined track, but staying in the air is more important. If the only chance to reach the goal means flying off course, this is what you have to do. You may never finally get to where you want to go, but you will give yourself the best chance of doing so if you know exactly in which direction you should fly at the top of each thermal. If you do get lost, do not wander about in hope; note a distinctive landmark and try to iden-

tify it on the map. Never attempt to find yourself by looking at, say, a town on the map and hoping to find it on the ground. You may be lucky, but it is most unlikely.

Wind

Throughout any cross-country flight you should try to keep track of the wind direction, because it can change. Factory chimney smoke, wind ripples on water and tall crops, and the shadows of cumulus moving over the ground are all useful. The wind can also become stronger or lighter and this will, of course, affect your rate of progress over the ground—and the rate at which landmarks come into sight.

Help from the compass

If a map is the primary navigational tool in a sailplane, the compass is next in importance. Its main use is to assist you to fly in a straight line in the desired direction. During a flight of several hours you will find that the direction in which you must fly will occasionally change, depending on the thermal distribution, but if you know what this direction should be, the compass will take you there.

If you use a compass simply to fly in a straight line, you read what it says when you are pointing in the right direction according to your land-

marks, and continue to fly on this heading until you wish to do something else. If you were flying straight towards your destination when you took the reading, any drift will have been taken into account.

However, you should know more about a compass than this if you want your navigational skills to equate with your soaring ability. Errors to which any compass is subject are described on page 36.

Flight planning

Although navigating a sailplane may appear to be a minute-by-minute affair, with frequent changes of heading—even destination—any flight has a better chance of succeeding if the pilot does some formal planning on the ground.

If, for example, you wish to fly round a 100 km triangle via two turn points, each leg of the triangle will be affected by the wind in a different way. The first leg may be into wind, the second cross wind, and the third with both a tailwind and some cross wind. On the first leg your groundspeed will be slow, on the second you will be drifted to the right of your track line, and on the last leg you will be blown home, but also a little to the left. The wind is blowing at 15 knots. How much should you allow for it on each leg?

The first leg, into wind, will be calculated on the achieved airspeed less the wind speed. 'Achieved' speed is an estimate of how much time will be spent flying straight, and how much circling while drifting with the wind at its speed. On this leg each thermal will drift you back the way you came, so your achieved speed is

not likely to be very high. If your straight flying cruise speed is 60 knots, the achieved speed on this particular leg will probably not be more than 25 knots. Subtract the headwind (15 knots) from this, and your ground speed for the first leg will be a mere 10 knots. You may think this is hardly worth the effort, but this leg is only 16 nautical miles long so it should not take you all afternoon: only about 1½ hours unless you keep losing your thermals.

The second, crosswind, leg may seem more difficult to work out, so use that basic navigational calculation: the triangle of velocities (see diagram). The speed used in drawing the triangle will have to be less than the inter-thermal cruise speed. For example, if you think the thermals will be good enough to permit you to cruise at 60 knots for half the time, with the other half spent circling, you

should use a speed of 30 knots to complete the triangle.

So far the flight time will be 1½ hours + 45 minutes = 2¼ hours.

Now for the last leg. It is almost, but not quite, downwind. Use the triangle of velocities again. However, later in the day, there are other considerations; the thermals may have become weaker or scarcer, and the wind may be lighter. Against this you will be both flying straight, and drifting when circling, in the direction of home. When straight you will fly at 60 knots, and you will circle at the wind speed—now 10 knots. If this last leg is 22 n.m. long and you spend half the time flying straight, and half circling, your achieved airspeed will be 35 knots. It will take you only 38 minutes. Total estimated time for the 54 nautical miles (104 km) triangle is 2 hours 50 minutes approximately. In actual fact it will not take you as long as this because you do not need to arrive home with more than enough height to make a safe circuit and landing. With the last leg downwind this final glide can be started perhaps half way along it. If, while gliding home you have any spare height, you can turn this into speed and get home faster (see page 129).

Planning a flight covers not only navigational calculations, but also the avoidance of controlled airspace, and weather considerations. For long cross-country flights, and certainly for record attempts, flight planning needs to be done both thoroughly and accurately.

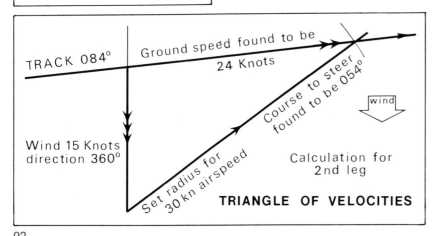

Field landings

How big is the best field? What grows in it?
Which way is the wind blowing?

This pilot has found no lift and will be on the ground in one minute's time. He turns towards the field in the foreground, nose well down to have plenty of speed ...

The field is not large enough to land on its flat top, so the pilot aims to come in low over the rising ground at the beginning of the field ...

Touch down. The pilot had enough spare speed to round out fully; he is actually touching tailskid first. Airbrakes are fully open ...

The problem with many field landings is to keep spectators out, so that crops are not damaged, and gates are closed.

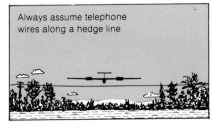

Always assume telephone wires along a hedge line

As soon as the new solo pilot starts chasing after thermals he increases the chances of ending up in a field, because he allows himself to be drifted out of reach of home while concentrating on staying in lift. There is nothing basically difficult about putting a sailplane safely into a strange field—it has always been an integral part of gliding—but it does need more than luck. Considerations include:

○ Selection of a good field; wind, slope, size, and surface.
○ Planning your approach into the field.

The second consideration also includes deciding on the height at which you will mentally stop trying to stay up and concentrate on getting down.

An expert pilot who knows his sailplane well may be both prepared and able to continue his hunt for lift

down to a few hundred feet above the ground, and may then land safely in a small field. But until you have done about twenty outlandings you should give yourself large margins for error and for unforeseen problems like invisible telephone wires along the approach hedge.

Height

There are three heights which become important whenever you are faced with the possibility of landing in a field. The first is the height at which you should not continue over country which offers little in the way of safe landing places. Certainly, to begin with, this should be about 2000 ft. In other words, at any time that you are down to 2000 ft you should stay over, or move towards good landing areas. The performance of your sailplane does not materially alter this figure. A medium performance school single-seater, with its low landing speed, needs a smaller field than a high performance ship. The latter has a better chance of reaching good landing areas, but with its higher landing speed and longer landing run it will need a bigger field. So, at first, take no chances: stay within reach of good landing areas. For example, in a school sailplane with a glide angle of 25:1 you will be able to fly just a distance of 15 km in calm air and no wind from a height of 2000 ft. Theoretically, this gives a circle of 30 km diameter in which to find a good field. These figures leave no margin of height for making the approach and landing, and in practice should be halved. If there is a wind, the circle of

Size, slope, and surface. *Below* The airfield this Schweizer 1-35 is flying from is not long. How big are the nearby fields? could you land in them? ...
Above right Which fields are flat? ...
Below right What is growing in these fields?

choice will be displaced downwind— so a good field upwind which looks quite close may not, in fact, be reachable.

If, at 2000 ft you still fail to find any lift, you should choose one or several actual fields by the time you are down to 1500 ft above the ground. You should not allow yourself to be drifted out of reach of at least one of these fields unless you can select a further satisfactory field. If necessary, this

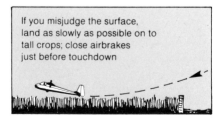

If you misjudge the surface, land as slowly as possible on to tall crops; close airbrakes just before touchdown

LANDING DOWN A SLOPE

A downslope of 3° is too steep, even using airbrakes

3°

process can be continued indefinitely. If you hit lift, use it, even if it gives only a few hundred feet (as long as when you are down to 1500 ft again you are able to select another good field).

The third and lowest height—1000 ft—is that at which, at least on your first outlanding or so, you deliberately stop thinking about thermals, and direct your eyes firmly at the ground. Do not forget that your altimeter is not necessarily giving you height above the fields that are underneath. If you are not yet practised in judging height, you may suddenly discover that the ground is closer than expected, and you have not even started to work out how to get the sailplane on to it.

Selecting the field

Size, slope, and surface. At first it is not easy to judge these qualities, but it is something that you can teach yourself when local flying. From the air choose any field in the vicinity of the airfield, and estimate how long it is into wind, how much it slopes, and what is growing in it. Then, after landing, go and inspect it. You may be surprised at how different it looks when seen from the ground.

Size

For your first few outlandings choose a really big field, or one that has great length into wind. Do not concern yourself with telephones or pubs—it is better to land the sailplane intact several miles from anywhere, than to

be within 100 metres of a telephone and a call home with news of a broken aircraft. If you see an electricity pylon anywhere around, look for other pylons to find where the cables are. If they run across the approach to your field, discard it; but if they are over or beyond the upwind end they are harmless, because unlike an aeroplane you cannot go round again! It is easy, of course, to say that the long run should be into wind, but it is often difficult to find out which way the wind is blowing.

Wind

Reliable signs are smoke, wind ripples on tall crops and water, and cloud shadows, although these will give you only wind direction at cloud height, which is usually slightly veered from the surface wind. Less reliable indicators include washing on lines near buildings. If you can see nothing to help you, think back to your take off into wind. Where was the sun in relation to the sailplane? If the flight has not lasted more than an hour or so, landing with the sun in the same position relative to the wings may assist you to some extent. Information on wind direction can also be obtained from the way your shadow is being drifted over the ground—but only when you are less than 500 ft up. It is only a last minute aid, but every bit of information helps to make your landing as near into wind as possible.

During the flight the wind may have become less strong, or it may have increased. Check on this as well, because although a stronger

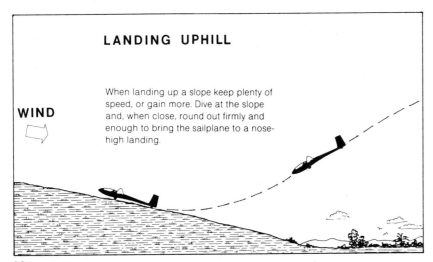

LANDING UPHILL

WIND

When landing up a slope keep plenty of speed, or gain more. Dive at the slope and, when close, round out firmly and enough to bring the sailplane to a nose-high landing.

wind gives you a shorter landing run, it also increases the chance of undershooting the field altogether.

Slope

It is essential to discover if the field slopes, because the glide performance of even a school sailplane is so good that almost any down slope will be too steep to put it on the ground before the far hedge, or ditch, is reached. It may even be better to land down-wind up a slope if you are faced with a choice. This is a real reason for choosing a field while you still have enough height to change your mind—if your field slopes down in the landing direction, discard it. Slope can be judged by relating your field to the surrounding landscape. Darker, damper ends or corners of fields are lowest. This also applies to streams and rivers, but not to canals, which may be up on an embankment like a railroad. If, from 1000 ft, it is obvious that a field slopes, it will be too steep to land on.

Surface

A smooth surface is best, either short grass, ground recently prepared for sowing, and in some countries dry lakes or beaches. Ploughed fields are unsatisfactory, particularly when the ridges are frozen; and those with bigger undulations, for drainage or caused by constant wind, can be almost guaranteed to do damage unless the sailplane is landed precisely along a ridge top.

The next problem is crops. Small seedlings do not harm, and need not be harmed if you land parallel to the rows, and keep spectators away. It is the bigger crops, such as corn or kale, which can do damage, usually because a wing tip catches first and swings the sailplane round while it is still moving quite fast. Again, inspect fields around the airfield, assess the crop type and size, and later look at it from the ground.

Animals are also a type of crop, be it a mobile one; and they vary in their habits. Cattle often stay still while the sailplane is landing, but afterwards arrive to discover if it is edible. Sheep stay and move in a flock, but may take no notice at all. Worst are horses, which are sensitive and may gallop about at random if they notice you on the approach. For choice pick an empty field.

Getting into the field

You are now at 1000 ft above the ground, have a good, big field within reach, and you know the wind direction and strength. How do you get down? In flying it is axiomatic that as far as possible you should avoid having to learn more than one new thing at a time, so plan to fly a normal circuit pattern. Allow only for the fact that the field is smaller than the airfield.

If you are still at a greater height than you need for your landing circuit, use it to fly over and around the field to make a further inspection. This will not only give a better idea of any slope, but will help you spot any rough patches or small obstacles that you had not noticed earlier. Now position the sailplane as though you are about to start a normal down-

wind leg, but a little further out from the upwind corner of the field. Fly the downwind leg making the same checks and assessments as usual, but particularly considering if you are at the right sort of height for where you are. If you think you are much higher than you ought to be, either edge away from the field so you fly a longer circuit, or simply use airbrakes to lower yourself down to a height that looks about right. If low, keep closer to the field, but you *must* start turning into wind while you still have enough height to complete the turn, even if you land with a slight cross wind. It is less expensive to break a wheel than a wing.

If all is going well turn on to base leg, but from a point a little more downwind than at home. Remember, the field is smaller than the airfield. Keep looking at where you intend to land, and again, if high, do not be afraid to use airbrake. Check that your approach speed is correct. Do not let it get too fast in your hurry to arrive safely on the ground, otherwise you will float further than you expect before touch down. On the other hand, if you are going to have to approach over tall trees, to the lee of which there may be turbulent downwash, make sure you have enough airspeed to fly over them.

Aim to land either in the middle of the field, or better, about a third of the way across it. If the field turns out to be enormous, do not change your mind to try to land near the edge, or by a gate. Go for the middle of the field as planned. Turn into wind on finals, use airbrakes as needed, and

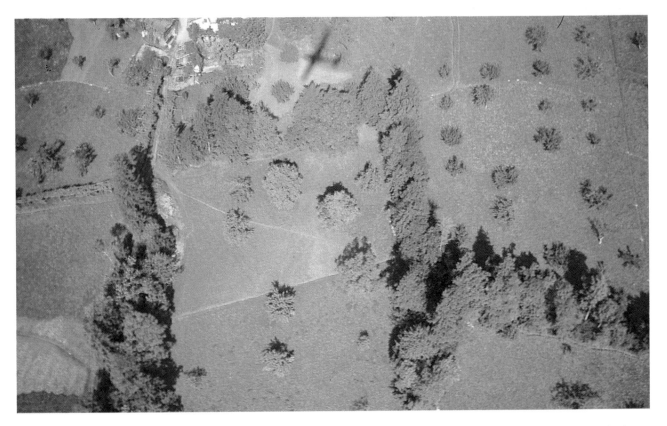

When below about 500 ft the drift of your shadow gives an indication of which way the wind is blowing.

concentrate on making a good landing. Let the sailplane run straight until it stops. Note the time, get out, park the sailplane by weighting the wingtip with the parachute (in·its bag), and decide how to set about the next two essential actions. These are:

○ informing your retrieve crew, or club, where you are; and
○ finding the landowner and explaining your arrival.

Will the pilot have enough height and speed to clear the fence?

The only landable place is the road. Is it wide enough?

If you have been using radio, your crew may already know where you are, but it is normally a rule that you telephone back as well, certainly with club sailplanes and in competitions. This is because positions given from the air are sometimes less reliable than believed by the pilot at the time! They may also be of little value for difficulties in reaching the field by road.

If your field selection was good, the

In empty country, like SW Texas, the highway may have to be both airfield and retrieve route.

landing was also likely to have been satisfactory; but sometimes at a late stage on the approach, when there is no question of being able to change to another field, the suspicion grows that all is not as anticipated. If that smooth-looking grass turns out to be tall, green corn, your best chance is to land as slowly as possible on top of it. Keep absolutely straight, and if your airbrakes project below the wing, close them just before you arrive on the crop. If you discover that the field is not level but slopes down away from you, the best way of stopping is to put the sailplane on the ground fast and to hold it there to grind off the speed on the wheel and skid, using the wheel brake (if any) as well. If this is still not going to stop you running into some hard obstuction, put a wingtip firmly on the ground so that the sailplane ground-loops, pivoting around the tip. These activities may cause some sailplane damage, but you have to accept this as the price for avoiding possible personal injury.

If, during the approach, you discover that the field slopes up into wind, there is no reason why you should not make a good landing, provided you come in with plenty of excess speed. You need this extra speed because, to land, it is necessary to rotate the aircraft through a greater angle than when landing on flat ground. So, increase speed, almost diving at the ground if the slope looks steep, and when you get close to the surface round out firmly and enough to bring the sailplane parallel to the slope—which may seem quite nose high. As it stalls, and it will do so more suddenly than on a normal landing, it will—or should—be in a landing attitude in relation to the ground, and just above it. If there is a wheel brake, apply it quickly to stop you running backwards down the hill. If no brakes, turn the sailplane across the slope with the last of any landing-run speed, which will not be much. If necessary get out quickly, grab a wingtip and hang on. With any luck the sailplane will swing round and stop. Now chock the wheel with a stone or seat cushion.

Because sailplane performance is so good, you may not have to land out very often. This is fine in terms of successful soaring, but may not give you enough field landing practice to become good at it. Although not as useful as landing in a strange field, you can help yourself by making every one of your airfield landings as accurately as you can on a predetermined spot. Sometimes, to make your practice seem more real, you can arrange to land in a normally unused part of the airfield. If you find that you are only doing about one outlanding a year, treat it as though it were the first you ever made—with all the margins against error that you can build in.

At this sort of height you should have good fields within easy reach.

What will this day's weather bring?

It is not necessary to become a meteorologist to be a good soaring pilot, but some understanding of the processes which go to make our weather—if only to avoid making a long journey to the airfield to find conditions unsuitable for flying. There are plenty of books about the weather, and a bibliography is given on page 141. These pages confine themselves to some of the ways cumulus clouds behave, which are useful to the soaring pilot.

Thermals

Thermals start at ground level as bubbles of air which are warmer than the surrounding air because they have been in contact with hotter areas of ground. They are, therefore, lighter and start to rise. As a thermal

Early on a moist air day a new cumulus is born

One hour later there are small cumulus all over the sky, with similar cloudbase height.

rises it will expand and, by doing 'work', it will cool itself. The rate at which it cools (assuming that it neither receives nor gives up any heat to the surrounding air) will be 3C° per 1000 ft. This is known as the *dry adiabatic lapse rate* (DALR). Dry because there is no cloud, and adiabatic because there is no heat entering or leaving the system.

The thermal will go on rising, cooling at 3C° per 1000 ft until its temperature is the same as the surrounding air. The lapse rate of this environmental air varies, but typically is about 2C° per 1000 ft. If, therefore, the thermal started off 2C° warmer than the surrounding air, the two lots of air would be at the same temperature at 2000 ft. From this it will be apparent that a thermal which has little extra

warmth at ground level will not rise very high. It is when the sun and the ground are hot that thermals rise to much greater heights before reaching equilibrium with the surrounding air.

Sometimes, usually in anticyclonic (high pressure weather), subsidence in the upper atmosphere creates a layer of warmed air, called an inversion. When the rising thermal reaches an inversion which is warmer than itself, this effectively puts a lid on it. When pressure is high and the anticyclone is intensifying, the inversion may be as low as 2000 ft above the ground. This makes cross-country soaring difficult. In strong inversion weather thermals are often strong, but narrow and rough.

On summer mornings, after a cool

night with very light winds, radiation will have thoroughly cooled the air in contact with the ground. This layer of cold air is usually several hundred feet deep, with the air above it slightly warmer. It takes a little time in the morning for the sun to heat the ground sufficiently to break up this inversion and allow thermals to develop normally. In a big competition, with perhaps 80 sailplane pilots waiting to fly, such an inversion is frustrating if it does not disappear much before midday.

Cumulus

If there is no inversion, so that thermals rise without such hindrance, they will produce cumulus clouds near their tops, unless the air is very dry. The height of cloudbase will depend on both the temperature and the humidity of the air, because warm air is able to carry more moisture as invisible water vapour than can colder air. On a cool day with a moist airflow, cumulus will form much lower than on a hot day with drier air. As the rising air in the thermal cools, it will steadily approach the temperature at which it can no longer carry all of its moisture as vapour. When this saturation point is reached some of the water vapour will condense out into droplets to appear as cloud. Cumulus clouds will develop at approximately the same height all over the sky. This is called the *condensation level*.

Once the air in the thermal reaches condensation level, the water vapour condensing into droplets gives up heat. This alters the lapse rate within

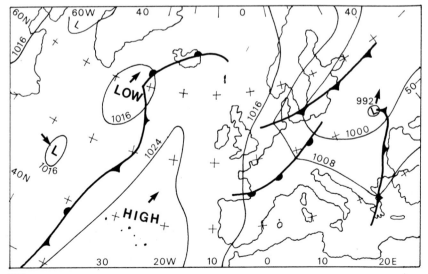

the cloud to about 1.5 °C per 1000 ft. It is known as the *saturated adiabatic lapse rate* (SALR). The cloud will continue to rise until its temperature has fallen to that of the surrounding air.

During the day, as the temperature rises, cloud base also rises because the now warmer air is able to carry its water vapour longer, and so higher. As the heat of the sun begins to decline during the afternoon cloud-base stays high, but thermals become generally weaker and less frequent. Now the wise pilot will try to stay as high as possible, using any scrap of lift he can find to do so. However, there are some exceptions to this, depending on the type of country below. During the day thermals readily depart from such sources as ploughed fields, or tarmac, which heat well and quickly, but not from woods and forests—these

absorb warmth only slowly. Late in the day as the air cools the absorbed heat in such sources becomes warmer than the surrounding air, and rises as large gentle thermals. Even in early evening residual warmth may rise from sheltered valleys or slopes, even shallow lakes. If the air is cooling rapidly through radiation, and there is no wind, this residual warmth may very gently rise enough to keep a sailplane airborne for a further half-hour or so. In windy countries, like Britain, this does not happen very often.

Thermals will still be able to develop when the sky is overcast, provided that enough heat gets through the cloud to warm the ground. The overcast may cover the sky with a veil of high cloud which, if a warm front is approaching, will gradually thicken and steadily reduce the incoming warmth until thermals are too weak

to be of use. Sometimes the high cover is broken, such as when isolated patches of high cirrus float across the sky, and the thermals will be weakened only from land which is in the cloud shadow. After the shadow moves on they will strengthen again.

On some days, if the air is moist, cumulus develop during the morning in the usual way, but at no very great height. As more and more cloud forms, and the existing cloud does not evaporate away as rapidly as it does in drier air, the cumulus run together to cover most of the sky. Now the sun's heat is largely cut off and few thermals develop until this existing cloud has, slowly, decayed. As blue patches begin to appear thermals start up again and produce more cloud. On some days this cycle repeats itself several times. When trying to soar cross-country it can be very frustrating. If you are forced to land in a field during one of the over-developed periods, you will be on the ground when, half an hour later, the sky is again filled with new and active cumulus—and luckier sailplane pilots.

One of the things it takes time to learn about cumulus is whether they are growing, with the thermal underneath still rising, or decaying—with nothing but sink as a welcome. When you start soaring, the sky may be full of cumulus all looking much the same; but the life of each individual cloud is only some 15 minutes, unless it is very large. After half an hour all the clouds in the sky will be different ones. For all practical purposes, at

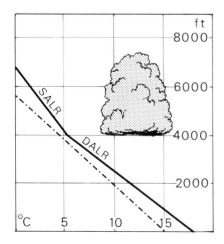

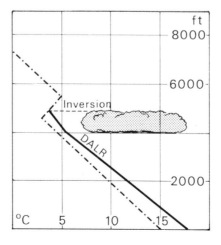

Good looking cumulus, but in the distance a huge thunderstorm is brewing, which will eventually destroy all ordinary thermals in its way.

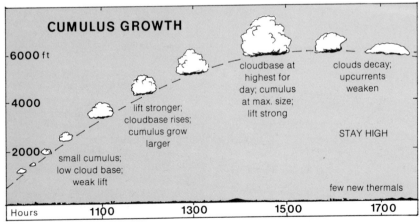

CUMULUS GROWTH

6000 ft

4000

2000

small cumulus; low cloud base; weak lift

lift stronger; cloudbase rises; cumulus grow larger

cloudbase at highest for day; cumulus at max. size; lift strong

clouds decay; upcurrents weaken

STAY HIGH

few new thermals

Hours 1100 1300 1500 1700

any given moment, half the clouds will be growing and the other half dying. Active clouds can sometimes be seen actually growing in size, but they are also fluffier and whiter, and have a darker, flatter—even concave—base. When they have reached maturity, and start to decay, the 'cauliflower' top subsides, the cloud begins to appear ragged, slightly yellowy, and the base less firm. There is no substitute for personal observation, though much of this can be done from the ground. Look at a cumulus cloud some distance away and watch it for the next

Big thunderstorms arrive with very strong and gusty winds, which can easily blow over a sailplane—almost without warning.

five or ten minutes to see how it changes. This is easier to do when the wind is light. In a wind of 25 knots at cloud height the cumulus you are so carefully observing will travel 7 or 8 miles and be hidden behind other clouds.

In the air, when you are trying to

decide which cloud to go for next, study the likely ones while you are still climbing in the previous thermal. This may give you quite a lot to do at once, but if you wait until you are close under cloudbase you will not be able to see any clouds properly: because all are at the same height they will be

obscuring each other when you are up there with them.

Cumulo-nimbus (cu-nb)

On some days the air may be unstable enough to encourage cumulus to grow tall, and even develop into cumulo-nimbus. These can really spoil an afternoon's soaring, because unless you are very skilled and the sailplane properly instrumented, you should not go anywhere near them, even if you are legally allowed to be sucked into cloud. A big cu-nb draws in air from all around, so for several miles in any direction there may be no other lift, and the air may be very turbulent. Thunderstorms also have a habit of growing outwards from themselves as well as moving along with the wind, so that a storm which you think will pass to one side may also grow quite quickly in your direction. In doing so it will swing the wind about, so unless you keep a close watch on the windsock you may end up landing inadvertently downwind. Do not forget that the winch, or tow car, cable could not have been better designed to act as a gigantic lightning conductor. If lightning is seen anywhere, or thunder is heard, stop launching.

Cloud soaring

Cloud soaring, once very popular, is prohibited in many countries because of controlled airspace demands. But if it is permitted, cloud should not be entered without understanding how powerful is the lift that some cumulus and cu-nb produce;

and certainly not without proper blind-flying instruments and the skill to use them. The risk of losing control of a clean and slippery sailplane, and then flying too fast, is real. Clouds produce stronger lift because the latent heat of condensation boosts the thermal strength in the cloud, so on a day when cumulus look like growing into thunderstorms, the wise pilot will leave a powerful thermal at least 1000 ft below cloud base.

Cloud streets

When the wind is strong cumulus may form into long lines, or streets, with lift for quite long distances under each cloud line. Occasionally this lift is continuous, but more often it is intermittent. If the street lies in the direction you want to go, well and good, but it is usually necessary to jump cross wind from one street to another to salve your navigational conscience. Since the lift lies under the clouds it should be expected that there will be downcurrents in between, so you need to cross these as quickly as possible. This is best done by deciding which bit of the cloud in the parallel street looks good, and when opposite it by flying straight across the gap at 90° to the lines of cloud. If you fly diagonally, you may think that you are gaining by going in a better direction, but you will spend a longer time in the downgoing air.

When the line of the cloud streets is such that the sun shines for some time on the long strips of sunlit ground between the cloud shadows, this tends to help perpetuate the street formation, with the lift being

more continuous under the clouds.

In very light winds thermals may come off a single source at fairly frequent intervals so that a line of separated clouds appears. This is not a true cloud street, but sometimes demonstrates well the life cycle of cumulus. As each new cloud grows, the earlier ones are dying away.

Sea breezes

On a day of strong convection, enormous masses of warmed air rise over the land. Between the thermals air sinks down more slowly, still possessing some residual warmth; but off the coast the sea is cool, as is the air over it. This coastal air flows in to replace, at low levels, the heated air rising over the land. Such sea breezes are strongest in the early summer, when the land heats readily but the sea is still cold, and are weaker in the late summer when the water has had time to absorb the summer's warmth. When there is strong convection over land the sea breeze may penetrate 30 km or so inland by the late afternoon. Over the ground newly covered by the cool sea air there will be few thermals. This is one of the considerations to take into account when plannng a cross-country flight in a small country, like Britain, or a narrow one, such as Italy.

There are occasions when a sea breeze generates excellent lift. This occurs when the land wind, for example from NE, converges wth a southerly or SE sea breeze. Cumulus develops along the convergence zone, and considerable distances can be flown under the line of cloud—which behaves in a similar way to a cloud street.

Sea breezes die away in the late afternoon or early evening, when the surface wind reverts to that of the prevailing weather system.

Cumulus in mountains

When cumulus develop in mountainous areas, such as the Alps, they are usually found over the crest of the mountains and not above the centre of the hot valleys, as might be expected. This is because thermals tend to flow up the sunny faces of the slopes, instead of rising freely from the valley. Whether cloud base will be above the peaks or among them depends on the humidity of the air.

Forecasting for yourself

If you talk to a top soaring pilot you will find that he knows an enormous amount about the weather. Much of this has been learnt from careful observation, from books, and from studying daily weather maps. Regular practice, as well as listening to forecasts, will soon help you to choose the best days to go flying, when soaring may be likely, and when to stay at home. Short-term forecasts, for the next six hours or so, can be made from what you can actually see in the sky, if you know what to look for. Try to relate forecasts to what you observe. Is the weather behaving as the met man thought, or is the expected deterioration going to arrive early—or late? The visible signs of the weather are there for you to see, and the good soaring pilot notices them automatically.

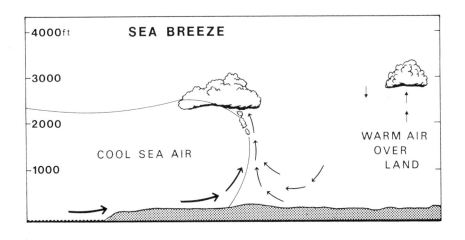

A cloud street developing in moist air conditions, so that cloudbase is low.

A well developed sea breeze convergence zone with big cumulus along it. Madras, India.

A warm front is approaching, and as the high cloud thickens thermals die away.

First cross-country

A beautiful day for a first cross-country.
Cumulus are well separated, the cloudbase is
high, and the wind light.

Your first soaring cross-country flight may be inadvertent, in that you just get too far from the airfield and have to land out; or it may be deliberate, to gain your Silver Badge. For the latter your intention is not only to fly out of reach of your home airfield, but to arrive at your goal. This has to be at least 50 km (31 miles) away. It is not a long distance to fly, but if it is your first cross-country, with your first out-landing in a new place, then 50 km or so will give you enough to think about. Although the Silver requirements may now allow you to obtain the 50 km distance during a much larger triangular flight, on a high performance sailplane, it takes away the essential ingredient of the straight flight Silver distance. For this you know before take off that you are definitely going to have to make an outlanding, so you fly mentally ready to do it. If you fly a triangle without any real outlanding experience, on a good sailplane, you tend to rely on its performance to return you safely to your home airfield. But if it does not, you will be faced with landing in a strange, and perhaps difficult, field without real thought as to how you will do it. This is a common way to damage an aircraft.

In planning your first cross-country flight you will discover that there are quite a lot of things to do, and information to obtain.

The weather Are the thermals going to be good, with the wind in the right direction—or may it become too strong for you? Is there any risk of sea breezes?

Your sailplane This may be a club

aircraft, so is it serviceable and properly equipped with parachute, barograph, etc? Will you need to carry personal ballast?

The flight What is the best time to launch, and at what minimum height are you prepared to leave the security of the home airfield? How are you going to navigate—have you got the right maps to cover the whole route, have you drawn your track line and is it clear of controlled airspace? How long will the flight take?

The landing (This is definitely going to be somewhere else.) What do you know about your intended destination? If a gliding club, how do they launch (so you know what to look out for)? Whereabouts on the field should you land? Does the club know that you are trying to get there, or is it necessary to inform them? Have you got a blank landing certificate for signature?

And if you do not get there? Is there any area on the route which is bad for landing? Are there hills or areas of high or rough ground on the way? Can you remember what you were taught about selecting a good field—size, slope, surface, etc?

What are the telephone numbers you may need and do you have telephone money?

The retrieve How are you going to get home again? Does your sailplane have a serviceable trailer (important if it is club equipment used by other people)? Who is going to retrieve you? Will they use their car, a club vehicle, or yours? Do the lights work—including trailer lights, etc?

Much of this should be planned,

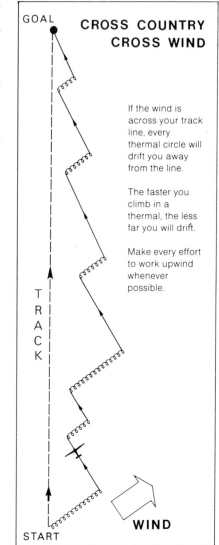

CROSS COUNTRY CROSS WIND

If the wind is across your track line, every thermal circle will drift you away from the line.

The faster you climb in a thermal, the less far you will drift.

Make every effort to work upwind whenever possible.

GOAL

TRACK

START

WIND

The 15 m span Libelle has an excellent all-round view for the pilot.

and checked, in advance, because the short time before take off should be spent in working out how best to make the flight, not in telephoning around to your friends for a crew, or fixing the trailer tow bar.

Flight planning

Lay out your map, draw your track line on it, and study the route for landmarks, way points, controlled air space, and any difficult or highly populated areas along the way. Now check the wind direction. For this first, straight flight it is preferable to have it directly on your tail, helping you along by adding to the ground-speed. More likely, it will be somewhat across the track and may drift you off your line. If so, you will need to head more towards the wind between thermals to counteract being blown downwind while circling up in them. So what good landmarks are there upwind of your track that would make useful references?

What is your destination airfield going to look like as you approach it—maybe without much height? Does it have runways and prominent hangars, or is it just a grass field with a nondescript shed? Is there a large town, or obvious road junction, nearby and how does the airfield lie in relation to it? What is the direction you wish to fly, and what will be your compass heading?

Have a really good look at the sky. It is now 10.00 hours, and the flight should take two hours at most—if you get there! So what time should you take off? If the day stays good, it would be right to take off an hour,

possibly two hours, before the strongest part of the thermal day. You would then land about an hour after it has passed its best. In other words, you make the flight using the peak period of the day. But is the day going to stay good? As well as listening to the forecast, and checking for yourself that the pressure is reasonably high (say 1025 mb or more), your own eyes can tell you most of what you need to know. So look.

Firstly, is any high cirrus cloud visible, particularly coming up over the horizon in a local bad weather direction, or is the upper air clear of any significant cloud? Are there signs yet of cumulus? If so, do they look as though they will soon over-develop and cover the sky to cut off the sun, or are they small, well separated, and have the appearance of staying that way? What conclusions have the more expert pilots arrived at—are other pilots preparing their sail-planes, or is there a noticeable lack

of interest in taking them out of their trailers?

So far so good, but what about the wind? There is a bit of a cross wind, but it is only light—10–12 knots, with no serious evidence of strengthening. Everything seems fine; just the day to go. But what about visibility? How can you check it? There is nothing in sight from ground level even 15 miles away; but you can see hills you know are 10 miles off, and they are clear. So visibility is at least 10 miles, probably better.

With your basic planning completed you decide to take off at 12.30, and go to have an early, light lunch and get some refreshments to carry on your journey.

The flight

You take off on time, and release from aerotow at 2000 ft two miles upwind of the airfield; your watch tells you it is 1240. There is no thermal

113

where you are, so you go to join a sailplane circling under a good-looking cloud a short distance away. Arriving at about 200 ft lower you find lift at once, and start to circle in the same direction as the sailplane above you. This is to the right, the direction in which you turn less well; and you remind yourself to practise turns this way. Suddenly the vario needle drops back and the audio goes quiet. You know the thermal is still there, but you are not in it. Then you notice that the sailplane above you, which is still rising, is further under the cloud than you are, so perhaps you turned too soon. You straighten up and fly so that the other sailplane is more overhead, and you start to circle again. Immediately the vario needle flicks up to 4 knots (2m/sec) and the audio pipes up again. This time you must be more careful, and you are. With a little adjustment you get nicely centred in the lift, which improves to 6 knots. The altimeter winds itself up to 3000 ft and the thermal is still working for you. Then the other sailplane straightens up and departs, increasing its speed to slip away into the distance. You also straighten up, and almost start to follow when you realise that it is not going your way. Half-in and half-out of the lift now, you do a couple more circles to look for your landmarks to find which way you should go. But at 4000 ft everything looks unfamiliar, and you are suddenly unsure of where you ought to be looking. Then you spot it—that town with the industrial chimney, and it all falls into place again.

Take the sailplane to the launch point. The day looks ideal.

You straighten up and go, looking ahead to where you could find your next thermal, and at the same time realising that every passing minute makes it less possible to return to that nice familiar field where you have done all of your flying. But enough of that; ahead are two clouds, one either side of track, and you, sensibly, decide to go for the up-wind one.

Opposite If you get low, choosing a field has absolute priority . . .

Opposite below But if you can stay airborne your goal looks good as you glide towards it.

Above Nicely in a thermal. You could do 150 circles on a two-hour flight.

Surprisingly, it is further away than you thought, and by the time you reach it the thermal is failing. After a few flickers of the vario the needle settles at 3 down, and you are right in the sink. The other cloud also seems now to be dying, but way ahead— perhaps too far—there is yet another cumulus; so you set off again and suddenly remember that you have not recently checked on your navigation. In a panic you look all around, but not quite where you expected it you spot landmark number 3, a big river bridge with a reservoir nearby. Reminding yourself not to forget again, you fly steadily on, losing height, towards the distant cloud which does not seem to come any nearer. You are now down to 2500 ft. Maybe you won't make it. You increase speed a little, not intentionally, but in an instinctive effort to arrive there faster. 2000 ft now—and what about being in reach of a good landing area? Reluctantly you look at the ground you do not yet want to be on; then look ahead at that still distant cloud. Without warning, the sailplane surges up and the audio howls. You have hit a thermal, and a good one, that you did not even know existed. Quick, start circling—no don't rush it, get properly in to the lift first; its good.

You take this thermal to 4000 ft before somehow losing it, and set off again. The compass heading is about what it ought to be, and landmark number 4 is visible, though way off to the left. So you must have drifted well downwind of your line; it will be even more of a windward slog to reach that goal airfield. Luckily, you find another thermal quickly, and at 4200 ft make a determined effort to make ground into wind. You nearly get back on to your intended line, but it is almost your undoing because you now cannot find any more lift. All the best clouds are in the direction you do not want to go. Again you have that dreaded sinking feeling; and watch with distaste the altimeter unwind itself to 2500 ft, then 2000 ft. Yes, there are good fields everywhere, but if it goes on like this you must choose one quickly. 1600 ft. You look at them all hurriedly. There are so many good ones it is difficult to select. 1300 ft. Yes, that big one over there—almost big enough to be an airfield, and it is flat. OK, so you settle for it. 1100 ft. Now you ought to change direction so you can use it. 1000 ft; the height you know you should forget about soaring and concentrate on landing, but it is difficult to do because you do not want to land one bit. With great reluctance you turn towards the field—and fly straight into another thermal. It is not strong like the last one, but it is not rough either. 2 knots up. You cannot resist the temptation to circle, and the chosen field slips out of reach. Guiltily, you know you must select another one—*now*; but it

is difficult to concentrate on staying in the thermal *and* checking out a field. And now the best fields are rather far away. Suddenly you realise what the instructor meant when he gave you those three decision heights. So you look at the fields again and choose one. It is not as good as the first, but it *is* large enough. Now the thermal is becoming erratic, so you concentrate even harder on staying in the best lift— and the field slides away. It is a relief when you realise that you are now up to 1600 ft; so the pressure is off—for the moment.

Slowly, gently, the thermal improves again, and as you climb through 2200 ft it is possible to think once more about navigation, except that you do not see anything that is recognisable. Suppressing the thought that you might be lost you work at gaining all the height possible. It is a lovely 4000 ft before the thermal dies, and you turn on to your

compass heading again. Now to have a good look round. The only prominent feature in view is a good-sized country town almost underneath with, in the distance ahead, a glittering line—the sea! It can't be. It is—so you must have passed your goal. Realisation dawns; that country town. It must have been the town near the airfield, so you flew right over the top of your destination without even noticing it! In a panic you turn to have another look at that town, and then to the south of it. There is the airfield, bright in the sunlight, and you are still at 3000 ft. With a great feeling of relief, because it is now so easy, you float around gently losing height, join the circuit as instructed, and even make a presentable landing. As you open the canopy, and the smell of warm, freshly-cut grass floods in, life is great. You have made your first cross-country.

Speed flying

For your first few cross-country flights you should avoid trying to hurry. It is more important to stay airborne and arrive, than to get there fast—or fail to do so. Later, when you attempt bigger task flights you will need to save valuable minutes and seconds to achieve your objective before the thermals die for the day. This is why soaring pilots concentrate so much on trying to fly fast.

To soar 500 km or more in a day it is necessary to try to pack as many kilometres as possible into each hour of flying, because the conditions, and the challenge, of each hour will be different. If you were making a straight distance flight downwind, as the pioneers did, it would pay to start

off as soon as the early thermals became usable, and try to stay airborne until they died away in the evening. For the first few hours of the flight, as you drifted along on the wind, your average speed would be low—only 20–30 knots—because the thermals would not yet have much strength, nor would they rise much more than 1000 ft or so. Later, as the heat of the sun increased, thermals would strengthen and rise higher, so that over the middle of the day you would achieve your highest average speed—perhaps 60 knots or more. In the late afternoon the strength and frequency of thermals would decline, and the average speed would again decrease. Finally, in the early evening

you would be just able to remain airborne, drifting along on what wind there was, until you finally landed. In this last hour your speed would again be little more than that of the wind, depending on how much of the time was spent circling. Apart from world distance record attempts, downwind distance flying is no longer practicable. A good pilot could end up more than 1000 km from where he started—and spend the next two days getting home again.

It is more sensible to make a long flight over an out-and-return or triangular course. At the end of the day the successful pilot is back home, and the unsuccessful one is not too far away.

The main difference between downwind and closed circuit flying is that in the latter some part of the course must be more or less into wind. If the pilot wants to make a big flight in the time available, he has to learn to fly fast all the time he is in the air. This not only means flying at high speed between thermals; he has to circle up in each thermal as efficiently as possible, since all the time he spends in it he will be drifting with the wind, at its speed and away from his goal. This is why, for closed circuit flying, the pilot prefers to use only the best part of the thermal day.

Best speed

To travel fast you have to fly at the best speed for each phase of the flight according to the conditions prevailing. On page 13 it was seen that the speed for minimum sink was

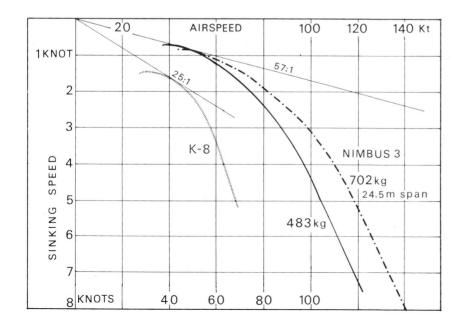

obtained when flying not far above the stall, and the best glide at a somewhat higher speed. Circling in a thermal at too high a speed is a positive disadvantage. Not only will

the sailplane climb more slowly than it need, but the pilot may not be able to make small enough circles to stay in the core. In such lift the pilot should fly at his minimum sink speed, and if the sailplane has flaps, these should be lowered a few degrees to improve

the slow flying qualities of the wing.

The instant the pilot leaves the thermal he needs to fly faster. This is, firstly, to pass quickly through any strong sink surrounding the thermal, and secondly, to cover the maximum distance over the gound in the right

A well judged final glide brings the sailplane across the finish line at maximum speed, perhaps 120 knots.

Water ballast is dumped if thermals weaken, and before landing.

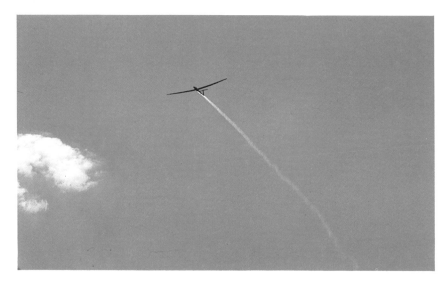

direction before he again has to find lift. The speed at which the sailplane is flown straight will vary. The optimum speed for best glide may be enough, or the pilot may want to fly much faster if the lift is very strong. Although higher speeds worsen the glide angle, the more rapidly the sailplane covers the ground, the less time it will spend in the sinking air between thermals. When the next one is found the pilot can soon regain the height lost through flying fast. Often the problem is to know what is actually the best speed to fly.

The MacCready ring

This is a movable ring which can be fitted to most variometers and which will show speeds to fly when set for prevailing thermal strengths. It is based on the performance curve, or 'polar', for the sailplane concerned, with the ring calibrated in knots (or km/h) in accordance with the polar and the scale of the variometer. The polar itself is a graph of the results of many test flights to measure the height lost, in calm air, at a series of different airspeeds.

Dolphin flying

On some good soaring days you may go faster by not circling at all. On meeting a thermal the pilot, who may be flying at 120 knots, pulls up steeply

When thermals are strong the sailplane is flown straight and fast.

MacCREADY RING

The ring was devised by Paul MacCready to fit on to the variometer. It assists the pilot to know at what speed he should fly in different lift conditions.
The ring is calibrated to suit the performance of the type of sailplane.

To fly the greatest distance

Set the ▶ mark on the ring to 0 on the vario. Adjust the airspeed until the ASI reading is the same as that indicated on the MacCready ring opposite the vario needle.
The airspeed adjustment has to be done progressively. If the sailplane flying at 50 knots now enters sinking air, the vario needle may indicate that the airspeed should be 70 knots. If airspeed is now increased, the sink rate will also increase, and the vario needle will show that a still higher speed is required. This little problem is overcome with practice.

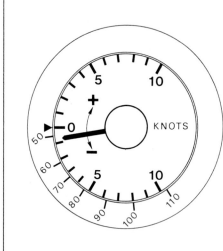

To achieve the highest average speed

To get the highest average speed on a classic circle, glide, circle type of cross-country. When setting off from each thermal it is necessary to estimate the rate of climb expected in the NEXT thermal.
Set the mark on the ring opposite the estimated rate of climb on the vario. In this case 4 knots. Proceed as before, adjusting the airspeed to equal that pointed out by the vario needle.

To use the MacCready ring effectively, the variometer must present the total energy of the sailplane, otherwise airspeed changes will give misleading information.
It is also necessary to use different rings for when the sailplane is full of ballast, or empty.

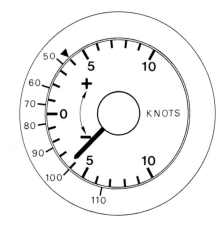

to convert speed into height within the confines of the thermal—which is also carrying the sailplane bodily upwards. The height gained in a pull up from 100 knots to 50 knots could be 350 ft. When the airspeed, through climbing, has fallen to that for minimum sink the pilot can either circle, if he still wants more height, or dive fast out of the thermal, and race on his way.

When flying cross-country with a series of sharp pull-ups and push-overs in each thermal, the pilot must realise that other pilots may be circling normally and must keep an extra careful look out.

Although the pilot aims to use the best part of the day for his flight, this does not always work out. All day he has been slower than he expected, and now is hanging on to every shred of lift to get home. When planning the route for a big flight there are many factors to be taken into account, but one of these is to plan to have the last leg more or less downwind. As long as it is possible to remain airborne the wind will help.

Water ballast

If a pilot hopes to fly fast to achieve a high cross-country speed, he wants his sailplane to be heavy to give him a higher wing loading. This will give best glide angle at a slightly higher airspeed—though at the cost of a worsened minimum sink rate. The best way to increase the weight of the sailplane is to carry water ballast which can be dumped quickly and safely for those on the ground.

On days of strong thermals the

Filling up with water ballast is a morning chore for the crew. 120 kg of water could come better from a hose – if there was one.

heavy sailplane will climb in them moderately slowly, but this disadvantage is less than the benefit gained when accelerating, and flying, at high inter-thermal speeds. If thermals weaken, ballast will be dumped. The pilot will now be able to climb faster in the weaker thermals, but will not be able to fly so fast between them without deterioration of his glide performance.

This relationship between airspeed, thermal strength, wing loading, and wind component needs to be well understood if the pilot wants to get the most from his soaring. But it will be of little use if the pilot is not able to control his aircraft with precision. Practice in this cannot begin too soon.

Competitions

Competitions have been a popular part of soaring, ever since the first glider pilots competed with each other to see who could stay up longest in hill lift. Later, competitions changed to find which pilot could soar the longest distance from his contest launch; and now the winner is the pilot who flies fastest round a set course of several hundred kilometres. Common throughout all this is the challenge of finding and using the energy in the air better than the other pilots—and some of them are very good indeed. In world championships several pilots may complete a 600 km triangle within seconds of the same elapsed time, with speeds of 100 km/h (54 knots) or more.

Local and regional competitions do not achieve such performances as these, but they are fun as well as being excellent ways of improving your flying. Not only will you be airborne every day for a week, weather permitting, so your flying improves, but in flying directly against others on the same task you have a good measure of how good you really are! It is easy, after soaring for a year or two to believe that you fly well; then you enter a regional competition only to find that maybe you are not as good as you thought. Usefully, you could also discover where you are going wrong.

Above Briefing each morning gives pilots and crews all the task and weather information needed.

Below Sailplanes on the grid at a world championships. (Paderborn, FRG)

Early morning. The crew prepares the sailplane in the sunshine . . .

Opposite above Position it at its numbered mark on the grid . . .

Opposite below Often thermals develop slower than expected, so everyone just waits.

The task flight for the day is set each morning at briefing and detailed information is given on expected weather. If there is more than one class of sailplane flying, it is usual to give a different task to each. This will be related to the performance of the sailplane, but it also reduces congestion in thermals and at turn points. Time of first take off will also be given.

After briefing, sailplanes are taken out to numbered spaces on the grid by their crews, from where they will be aerotowed up to a common dropping zone a mile or so from the airfield. The usual release height is 2000 ft, or 700 m.

The meteorologist chalks up the latest weather on the briefing board.

Wing covers are left on until just before launching to protect the wings from dust and flies . . .

Contest flights are timed from start to finish line, and controlled at turn points by photographs taken by the pilot. He has two cameras (in case one fails) fixed in the cockpit so that the pictures are taken through the left side of the canopy. When airborne, and ready to set off on the task, the pilot first photographs a ground clock (or is observed and timed across a start line). This ground clock consists of a series of panels changed at frequent and set intervals to correspond accurately to real time. The pilot's photograph of the panels tells the organisers the exact time at which he departed to fly the task.

The object now is to find and reach the turn points, photograph them from the correct sector, and return home to cross the finish line. The elapsed time of each pilot is then compared, and the fastest given maximum points—usually 1000—for the day, with the slower pilots scored in relation to the fastest. At the end of the competition the pilot who has amassed the highest total score is the

have not got around to doing—like changing a worn landing wheel tyre? If there are such jobs, do them; and then carefully clean and polish the whole aircraft. Finally, obtain and pack any spares you think you might need, including camera films—unless these are provided by the organisers.

The trailer There is usually not much wrong with a well-loved sailplane, because time is devoted to its care, but often this is at the expense of the trailer. So give this an extra good inspection, including a check of attachment of internal fittings, tow bar, brakes, and door locks and catches. If there is work to be done, do it. It is quite useless having your sailplane far from the take-off point just because the trailer broke down.

The retrieve car This may be yours or it may belong to your crew, but someone has to make sure that it will work well throughout the competition. The retrieve car also has a further important function: it is the base camp for the sailplane and its pilot and has to be equipped accordingly. This means VHF radio installed, possibly with a spare aerial (insurance against theft), road maps covering the whole contest area, and a duplicate set of air maps. These not only may have to act as spares for the pilot if he loses his, but can be useful for reference if there is difficulty in locating the pilot in his field. The retrieve car also needs a cool box for refreshments, particularly if the weather is hot; spare protective clothing, such as waterproofs and wellies, for that muddy field retrieve; and

Good crews are important and much appreciated by their pilots . . .

winner. If a pilot fails to complete the task he is scored only on the distance he has flown; without any speed score he does not get many points. Such is an outline of the competition structure, but it gives no idea of the fun.

When you think that you have done enough flying to try your hand at a competition, pick a local one for the first because there is much more to contests than just soaring, and it is sensible to minimise the number of new things you will have to think

about. Even flying over familiar country helps. In your first competition the need to win should not be paramount. There is obviously little point in entering unless you intend to do as well as possible, but the primary objective should be to learn. There is also little point in competing unless your sailplane, trailer, retrieve car, crew and yourself are in top condition, and this means thorough preparation.

The sailplane Is it properly serviceable, including instruments, turn point cameras, maps and parachute, or are there several little jobs that you

125

a good flashlight, with spare batteries, for finding that vital rigging pin you dropped in the long grass after dark. There will be other things which personal choice and experience will dictate, but the list should also include notebook, ball-point pens, telephone and car park money, and credit cards.

While pilots search the sky for thermals, crews may have little to do . . .

– or may have to look for their pilot in unlikely places.

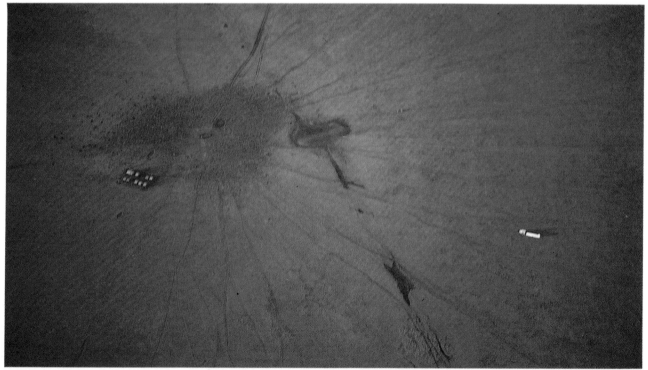

Final glide. It can look a long way without an engine.

Sometimes a sailplane arrives over the finish line alone – and sometimes in company . . .

But will this one make it home?

Turn point cameras are fixed on the left side of the cockpit, with pictures taken through the canopy . . .

Crew Although many pilots have only a single crew, there are great benefits in having two people especially if your crew has not done this job before and so may not appreciate just how much is involved. Retrieves may last well into the night—or, more boringly, there may be no retrieves at all. A good crew should nurse-maid the pilot to the extent that he can concentrate on the task in hand, particularly between briefing and take off. This means that the crew rigs and checks the sailplane, polishes it, takes it to the grid, and ensures that the pilot does not forget his maps, dark glasses, apples, or whatever else it is he needs when flying.

Yourself—the pilot Are you really looking forward to competing, or are you anticipating the contest merely as a relaxing week away from a tedious business schedule? Are you in good physical condition, or suffering from hay fever, too much food, or too little exercise? Are you now regretting having entered because you are scared you will make a fool of yourself? All these situations and reactions are normal, but it is sensible to think about them honestly, so that once the competition starts you can concentrate on flying well for the right reasons.

It is essential to read the contest rules carefully, and to understand them and the scoring system. Many pilots have lost for no better reason

The pilot takes a control photograph showing date and his sailplane number before take off.

than they had not flown the task correctly, because they had not studied the rules, or had not paid sufficient attention at briefing.

Having been given the task for the day this should be plotted on your map, and the effects of wind, thermal strength, and visibility considered. Make any notes that might be helpful, for example, on the chances of high cloud cover during the afternoon or that to complete the task at all you

will have to aim for an average speed of at least 80 km/h during the best part of the day. Try to think your way around the course, and study the map for problems. How near is any controlled airspace; are there any unlandable areas?

In the air you may be concerned at first about flying close to the large numbers of sailplanes that seem to be in 'your' bit of air, but this is one thing you should have anticipated. In thermals you will discover the need for disciplined flying and keeping a really good look out—which gives you less time in which to concentrate on flying accurately. Next, you have to decide on the best time to cross the start line, or take your start photographs. Not unnaturally, to begin with, you tend to follow other more experienced pilots, but this is no bad thing to do as other sailplanes ahead will act as thermal markers, which may give you a little less to do.

In your first competition you will discover that one of the most difficult things is to take correct photographs of the ground clock and turn points. Not only will you find it hard to get in exactly the right position, according to the rules, but other sailplanes will be quite close, with their pilots trying to do the same thing. This is something else that you can practise prior to the competition. If you take photographs locally of ground features and study the film results, you will learn better how to position yourself

to get the turn point clearly in your picture. This will make it easier to slot in with other competitors.

Navigation often seems easier in a contest because of the number of sailplanes going the same way, but you must still do your own map reading as well. If you rely on following other pilots, Murphy's law will see to it that you follow the only pilot who is lost!

If by now you have managed to soar around the course and are now on the final leg towards home, you must start thinking about when you are going to begin the final glide.

The final glide

If the object of the flight is to complete the course at the fastest speed, there will come a time when no more lift is needed to reach the goal. The sailplane can now be flown straight towards home to arrive over the finish line with only enough height to land. So how do you know when you need no longer spend time circling, or how high you should be, or how fast you can fly? If the thermal is weak it will pay to start the final glide as soon as you are high enough to just reach your goal flying at a slow speed, whereas if it is strong it will be better to climb higher and then fly home at a faster speed.

The problem can be solved by intuition, or by a graph, slide rule type of calculator or a computer, each based on the polar for the sailplane

Nimbus 3 pulls up victoriously over the finish line.

type. With inputs of distance to go and head or tail wind component, the minimum height to leave the thermal can be determined. In addition, the device can show optimum heights to depart for various rates of climb. If the lift weakens to this value you should set off. Once you have decided to go, the past is history. You can fly with the MacCready ring set at the rate of climb achieved in the last thermal, slowing down in lift, and increasing speed in sink, and monitoring your progress. If you fly into a large area of sink and it becomes doubtful if you can reach home, you must decide whether it is better to fly in hope, or forget about the final glide and find more lift. Turbulence and inaccuracies in your flying will also take their toll of performance.

At this point a practical problem may creep in. From where you are able to start your final glide, you cannot see your destination because it is too far away. A Nimbus 3, for example, could reach its goal 75 km distant from 4500 ft, but if visibility is only 15km the pilot cannot see where he is trying to go for. This not only adds to the calculation problems on the way in, but even more to the navigational ones. Accuracy cannot be achieved unless the wind strength and the exact distance to be flown are known. For your first few final glides, because it all seems a complicated and worrying process, it will pay to come in high deliberately.

The score board has a continuous fascination for both pilots and crews.

Instead of aiming to arrive fast at 100 ft, get home at 300 or even 500 ft. If you appear as a speck in the sky to watchers below, so what. You have made it!

There are pilots who become so enthusiastic about competition flying that they enter as many events as they can. Some do it to try to work their way up to international level, while others are content with plenty of enjoyable and friendly flying.

Appendix 1: Units and conversions

Aviation has not done too well in simplifying the problem of mixing different units. Distance can be measured in nautical miles or kilometres, speed in knots (1 knot = 1 nautical mile per hour) or kilometres per hour, and height in feet or metres. If you are familiar with both systems, so much the better, but if not the table below should help you make any necessary conversions.

It is useful to remember that 1 knot equals approximately 100ft/min
1 knot = 0.515 m/s
1 m/s = 1.94 knots

Length
1 foot (ft) = 0.305 m
1 inch (in) = 25.4 mm
0.001 in (1 'thou') = 0.025 mm
(= 25 microns)
1 metre (m) = 3.28 ft
1 millimetre (mm) = 0.0394 in
(= approx. 40 'thou')

Area
1 ft² = 0.0929 m²
1 m² = 10.76ft²

Volume
1 in³ = 16.38 cm³
1 cm³ (1 cc) = 0.0612 in³

Weight
1 pound (lb) = 0.454 kg
1 kilogram (kg) = 2.205 lb

Wing loading
1 lb/ft² = 4.88 kg/m²
1 kg/m² = 0.205 lb/ft²

Fuel capacity

Imperial Gal (used in UK)		U.S. Gallon		Litre
Gal		U.S. Gal		1
1	=	1.20	=	4.54
0.833	=	1	=	3.78
0.220	=	0.264	=	1

I.C.A.O. ALPHABET

A	Alpha
B	Bravo
C	Charlie
D	Delta
E	Echo
F	Foxtrot
G	Golf
H	Hotel
I	India
J	Juliet
K	Kilo
L	Lima
M	Mike
N	November
O	Oscar
P	Papa
Q	Quebec
R	Romeo
S	Sierra
T	Tango
U	Uniform
V	Victor
W	Whiskey
X	X-ray
Y	Yankee
Z	Zulu

Appendix 2: Aerobatics

Most sailplane pilots prefer soaring to aerobatics, and many high performance sailplanes are not ideally suited to being turned upside down.

Aerobatics can be divided into two groups: positive g manoeuvres, such as loops; and those involving negative g, like slow rolls. Positive g aerobatics are relatively simple, and can be taught on most school two-seater gliders whereas rolls or inverted flying demand proper training on a sailplane designed for this type of flying.

At some stage in a pilot's flying career it is no bad thing to have some aerobatic training. It leads to greater precision in handling the aircraft, and enables the pilot to become familiar with controlling unusual attitudes and situations, such as could be met in extremely turbulent air.

The two most popular positive g manoeuvres are the loop and the chandelle. The latter is similar in appearance to a stalled turn, except that the sailplane is not actually allowed to stall. If it does, and slides tail first even for a few seconds before flipping over, nose down, the control surfaces may be pushed hard against their stops and damaged. If a pilot, with 50 + hours in his log book and in current practice, wants to try loops without some dual instruction, he must be clear before starting as to what he is trying to do. The problems are stalling inadvertently on the top of the loop, and flying far too fast when coming out at the bottom. As a minimum he should get a good briefing from his instructor or a skilled *sailplane* aerobatic pilot.

It should not be necessary to emphasise again that the pilot should have a good look round for other aircraft before commencing any manoeuvre and should the sailplane be accelerating fast in a dive, open the *airbrakes immediately*. It is usual that more height than expected will be lost when a pilot first begins doing even simple aerobatics, so they should be started above 3000 ft— and in smooth air.

Never attempt negative g aerobatics, or inverted flying, without instruction in a two-seater which is certificated for such manoeuvres. In many countries it is compulsory to fit an accelerometer (to measure the g applied) in any sailplane used for aerobatic training.

There are FAI World Championships for glider aerobatics. These are looked after by the FAI Aerobatic Committee, CIVA.

Appendix 3: International FAI Gliding Badges

STATUS OF BADGES

The FAI badges are standards of achievement which do not require to be renewed. The qualifications are the same in every country.

The silver badge is intended primarily to develop the self-reliance of the new soaring pilot. The distance flight should be flown without navigational or other assistance given over the radio (other than permission to land on an airfield) or help or guidance from another aircraft.

QUALIFICATIONS AND REQUIREMENTS

Silver badge
Distance: a straight course of at least 50 km.
Duration: at least 5 hours.
Height: 1,000 metres gain.

Gold badge
Distance: 300 km.
Duration: 5 hours.
Height: 3,000 metres gain.

Diamonds
There are 3 Diamonds:
– Diamond distance: 500 km.
– Diamond goal: 300 km over a triangular or out-and-return course, which must be completed.
– Diamond height: 5,000 metres gain.
Diamonds may be worn only on a silver or gold badge.

1,000 KM badge
A distance flight of at least 1,000 km.

BADGE	Silver	Gold	Diamonds to silver and gold badges	1,000 km
Duration	5 hours	5 hours		
Gain of height	1,000 m.	3,000 m.	5,000 m.	
Goal			Completed out-and return or triangle of 300 km	
Distance	50 km	300 km	500 km	1,000 km
course alternatives				

Silver and gold badge

Three diamonds badge

1,000 km badge

FAI GENERAL CONDITIONS

The pilot must be alone in the glider on each flight.

A flight may count towards any badge or diamond for which it fulfils the conditions.

FAI flight declarations must be complied with except that distance may be claimed from an uncompleted triangle provided that the qualifying distance is flown and the glider is landed not more than 10 km off the line of the last leg. Flights qualifying for badges shall be controlled in accordance with FAI requirements. For silver distance the height difference between release and the landing place shall not exceed 1% of the distance flown.

Appendix 4: The British Gliding Association Bronze Badge

The Bronze badge is used in Britain as the level of proficiency necessary before a pilot is permitted to fly cross-country. It is the equivalent of a pilot licence.

Flying test

1 Two soaring flights, each at least 30 minutes when launched by car, winch or bungie, or 60 minutes after release from an aerotow to a height not exceeding 2,000 ft. Landing must be normal, and within the boundary of the landing field as specified by the Instructor in charge. The candidate must be alone in the aircraft for each flight. Each soaring flight must be under the supervision of a BGA Instructor or Official Observer, who must complete and certify the report form. The evidence must be by a barograph trace to the satisfaction of an Official Observer or alternatively may be by continuous visual observation.

2 A minimum of two flights in a dual control glider with the CFI or a nominated Full Rated Instructor. The Instructor is to satisfy himself that the candidate is proficient in the following exercises:

a Well co-ordinated and accurate general flying, especially the keeping of a good look-out.

b Understanding and recognition of the symptoms of a stall, incipient spin and full spin, followed by the correct recovery. If sufficient height is not available for a full spin, then practice to the incipient stage is acceptable, though not ideal.

c Two field landings into a field or, if a suitable field is not adjacent to the Club site, into a marked area of the airfield. The altimeter should be covered or the millibar scale offset for this practice. If a marked area of the airfield is used, it must be so chosen that there is little, or no undershoot, and that the circuit and approach do not coincide with the normal circuit and approach to the airfield. Where a suitable two-seater is not available, the field landings *only* may be flown solo.

Ground test and general requirements

1 Complete the Bronze Badge written examination paper, correctly.

2 Have received a comprehensive ground briefing on cross-country techniques and field landings. The briefing is to be given by a Full Rated Instructor.

3 At least 50 solo flights in a glider, or at least 50 hours PI in powered aircraft plus 20 solo flights in a glider.

4 The flying and ground tests must all be completed within the 12 months prior to the application.

Appendix 5: World Records

These are the world's best performances, as at 1.1.85. There are also world records for women, motor gliders, and for two-seaters in all categories.

Distance in a straight line
Hans Werner Grosse	FRG	ASW 12	25 April 1972	1,460.8 km

Straight distance to a goal
S H Georgeson	New Zealand	Nimbus 2		
B L Drake	New Zealand	Nimbus 2	14 January 1978	1,254.26 km
D N Speight	New Zealand	Nimbus 2		

Out and return distance to a goal
T L Knauff	USA	Nimbus 3	25 April 1983	1,646.68 km

Distance around a triangular course
Hans Werner Grosse	FRG	ASW 17	4 January 1981	1,306.9 km

Absolute altitude
Paul F Bikle	USA	Schweizer SGS 123E	25 February 1961	14,102 m

Gain of height
Paul F Bikle	USA	Schweizer SGS 123E	25 February 1961	12,894 m

Speed over 100 km triangular course
I Renner	Australia	Nimbus 3	14 December 1982	195.3 km/h

Speed over 300 km triangular course
Hans Werner Grosse	FRG	ASW 17	24 December 1980	158.67 km/h

Speed over 500 km triangular course
Hans Werner Grosse	FRG	ASW 22	20 December 1983	159.64 km/h

Speed over 750 km triangular course
Hans Werner Grosse	FRG	ASW 17	6 January 1982	143.63 km/h

Speed over 1000 km triangular course
Hans Werner Grosse	FRG	ASW 17	3 January 1979	145.33 km/h

Speed over 1250 km triangular course
Hans Werner Grosse	FRG	ASW 17	8 December 1980	133.24 km/h

In the other categories outstanding performances include:

Two-seater distance in a straight line Held by Dick Georgeson and his wife, Helen, who flew a Janus C 993.76 km in New Zealand on 31 October 1982. This also beat the world goal flight record

Two-seater absolute altitude L E Edgar and H E Klieforth reached 13,489 metres in wave in a Pratt-Read PR GI on 19 March 1952. This record has now stood for 33 years.

Women's speed over 100 km triangular course This stands at 139.45 km/h by Sue Martin, Australia, on 2 February 1979. She also holds the speed records for the 300 and 500 km triangles.

Motor glider distance around a triangular course F Rueb, FRG, holds seven world motor glider records, his best performance being the triangle distance. On 31 December 1979 he flew his Nimbus 2 M 1,013.21 km.

Appendix 6: World Gliding Championships Classes

World Championships are normally held in all three Classes, though Continental and National Championships may take place in one or two Classes only. Each Class is a contest in its own right, declaring its own champion.

The open class
No special rules.

The 15 metre class
The only limitation is a maximum span of 15,000 mm.

The standard class
Obligatory requirements:

a Wings. The span must not exceed 15,000 mm. Any method of changing the wing profile other than by normal use of the ailerons is prohibited. Lift increasing devices are prohibited, even if unusable.

b Air brakes. The glider must be fitted with airbrakes which cannot be used to increase performance. Drag parachutes are prohibited.

c Undercarriage. The undercarriage may be fixed or retractable. The main landing wheel shall be at least 300 mm in diameter and 100 mm in width.

d Ballast. Water ballast which may be discharged in flight is permitted.

Because sailplanes filled with water ballast are very heavy, they require both a large airfield and powerful towplanes. For safety reasons organisers of championships may declare a maximum all up weight for each class, which may be less than that permitted by the Certificate of Airworthiness of the sailplane. For the Open Class this is 750 kg or less.

FAI World Championships are held every second year in a different country, and last 16 days. The number of sailplanes entered is usually between 80 and 100.

Appendix 6A

Some representative gliders from 1935–1985

Type	year	span	wing area	aspect ratio	empty weight	max. weight	wing loading at max. weight	glide ratio	min. sink
		m	m²		kg	kg	kg/m²		m/s
Minimoa (wood)	1936	17	19.5	16	200	298	15.3	26	0.6
Meise (wood)	1938	15	15	15	160	255	17	25	0.67
Skylark 2 (wood)	1953	14.6	13.4	16	191	272	20.3	27	0.67
Ka-6 (wood)	1955	15	12.4	18.1	185	300	24.2	31	0.63
Libelle (glass)	1967	15	9.8	23	185	350	35.7	38	0.6
LS-6 (glass)	1984	15	10.5	21.4	250	525	50	40+	0.6

Appendix 7: Addresses and organisations

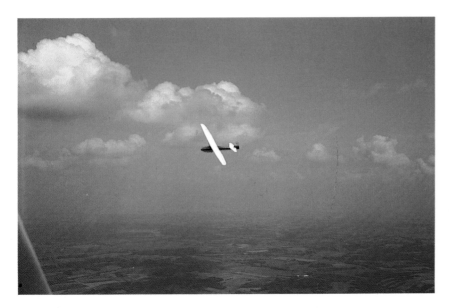

A vintage Prefect, built in 1948, floats in the summer sky. All over the world historic gliders are lovingly restored.

The Fédération Aéronautique Internationale (FAI)
6 rue Galilée, 75782 Paris cedex 16, France.

The British Gliding Association
Kimberley House, Vaughan Way, Leicester, LE1 4SE, England.

The Soaring Society of America
P O Box 66071, Los Angeles, California 90066, USA.

The Gliding Federation of Australia
130 Wirraway Rd, Essendon Airport, Victoria 3041, Australia.

The Vintage Glider Club of Great Britain
'Wings', The Street, Ewelme, Oxfordshire, England.

The Civil Aviation Authority
Aviation House, Kingsway, London WC2, England.

The British Gliding Association
The BGA is the national organisation which looks after gliding and soaring throughout the United Kingdom, and has done so since 1930. It is responsible for pilot standards, through its Bronze badge and the FAI international badges, for airworthiness and certificates of airworthiness, and for encouraging gliding clubs.

Its magazine, *Sailplane and Gliding*, is published every 2 months. The editorial office address is 281, Queen Edith's Way, Cambridge, CB1 4NH, England.

The Fédération Aéronautique Internationale (FAI)
Internationally, all sporting flying is looked after by the FAI, which is the world authority for the control and encouragement of records, championship organisation and rules, and pilot proficiency standards. The national aero clubs of each country make up the membership of the FAI. The special international committee for gliding in FAI is the CIVV (Commission Internationale de vol à voile), to which each member country of FAI is entitled to send a delegate. Correspondence to FAI should be directed via the National Aero Club. In Britain this is the Royal Aero Club, Kimberley House, Vaughan Way, Leicester LE1 4SE.

OSTIV (The International Scientific and Technical Gliding Organisation)
OSTIV is closely associated with the FAI Gliding Committee, CIVV, and holds its technical congress at the site of the World Gliding Championships every two years. Technical papers are welcome. Address: Institut fur Physik der Atmosphare, 8031 Oberpfaffenhofen, Post WESS-LIGN/OBB, FRG.

Appendix 8: Rules of the air

Rules for the avoidance of collision

The rules for avoiding head-on, converging, or overtaking collisions are international. For ridge soaring and circling in thermals there may be local special rules that apply only to sailplanes.

The international rules are based on the principle that the aircraft which has right of way shall maintain its course and speed, as follows.

Converging When two aircraft are converging at approximately the same altitude, the aircraft which has the other on its right shall give way.

Meeting head on When two aircraft are approaching each other head on, or approximately so, each shall alter course to its right.

Overtaking Overtaking aircraft shall at all times keep out of the way of the aircraft which is being overtaken by altering course to the right. In the UK a sailplane overtaking another sailplane may alter its course to the right or to the left.

Coming in at last light. Legally, night starts 30 minutes after sunset.

Whereas aeroplanes shall, when converging, give way to aerotows and sailplanes, and sailplanes shall give way to balloons, it is nevertheless the responsibility of all pilots at all times to take all possible measures to avoid collision.

Landing When landing the lower aircraft has right of way, but it may not cut across the path of another aircraft which is on the final approach. If the pilot is aware that another aircraft is making an emergency landing he shall give way to it.

Aerobatics Aerobatics are prohibited over congested or urban areas, or within controlled airspace without the consent of Air Traffic Control.

Following roads and railways In the UK aircraft following roads or other landmark lines shall keep such landmarks on their left.

Minimum age In the UK the minimum age to fly solo is 16.

Dropping of objects Nothing shall be dropped from a sailplane, other than persons by parachute in an emergency, articles for the purpose of saving life, ballast in the form of fine sand or water, or tow ropes on airfields.

Accidents An accident which causes injury, or substantial damage to an aircraft, must be reported to the police and to the Civil Aviation Authority Accidents Branch.

Air Law in the UK

The Air Law which the sailplane pilot must know is contained in the *Air Navigation Order (ANO)*, the *Air Pilot*, *The Aeronautical Information Publication (AIP)* and *NOTAMS*. All are available from CAA.

Before any pilot begins to fly across country on his own he must learn about the many regulations which will affect him—including ground signals and lights, visual distress signals, the carriage of dangerous goods, drunkenness in aircraft, notification of accidents, and most importantly, about where he may or may not fly.

Controlled airspace

This includes: CONTROL ZONES (areas which extend from the surface upwards to a defined level); CONTROL AREAS (these start from a defined level and extend upwards to a further defined level); AIRWAYS (corridors of controlled airspace linking major airports). A *purple airway* is a temporary airway for the passage of royal flights. For all practical purposes a sailplane may not enter controlled airspace without permission, except for crossing airways VMC.

Prohibited areas

Atomic Energy Establishment areas have a radius of 2 nautical miles and extend 2,000 feet upwards. *Danger Areas* are used for military firing, including the use of pilotless target aircraft. Although it is not always an offence to enter them it may be extremely unwise. *Restricted or hazardous* areas include almost anything from high-intensity radio transmission areas, free-fall parachute areas and bird sanctuaries.

Aerodrome traffic zones

Every aerodrome has a traffic zone (ATZ), extending from the surface to 2,000 feet within 1.5 nautical miles of the airfield boundaries, which may not be entered without permission. Some aerodromes also have a special rules zone (SRZ). All aircraft have to conform to air traffic control (ATC) instructions while within the area. Some military aerodromes have a traffic zone (MATZ), which has a 5 nautical mile radius with a projecting stub 4 miles wide aligned with the main approach and extending to 3,000 feet.

VFR and IFR

All flights must be conducted in accordance with either Visual Flight Rules (VFR) or Instrument Flight Rules (IFR).

Visual Meteorological Conditions (VMC) are those which enable the pilot to maintain VFR Briefly, they are:

a *Above 3,000 ft.* Remain 1 n.m. horizontally and 1,000 ft vertically from cloud, and in a flight visibility of at least 5 n.m.

b *Below 3,000 ft.* If flying at less than 140 knots, clear of cloud, in sight of the surface and in a flight visibility of at least 1 n.m.

Instrument Meteorological Conditions (IMC) are those when the pilot cannot comply with VMC.

The Air Law requirements are given in CAP 85, issued by CAA.

Appendix 9: Bibliography

Beginning Gliding, Derek Piggot (A & C Black)

Gliding, Derek Piggot (A & C Black)

Going Solo, Derek Piggott (A & C Black)

KTG Gliding, Ann Welch (A & C Black)

KTG Hang Gliding, Ann Welch (A & C Black)

Meteorology for Glider Pilots, C E Wallington (John Murray)

New Soaring Pilot, Welch and Irving (John Murray)

Pilot's Weather, Ann Welch (John Murray)

The Complete Hang Gliding Guide, Noel Whittal (A & C Black)

The Story of Gliding, Ann Welch (John Murray)

Understanding Gliding, Derek Piggott (A & C Black)

Index

The American Schweizer 1–35 is metal, and unlike glass fibre sailplanes is painted a bright colour.